THE LIPSTICK
PRINCIPLES

THE LIPSTICK
PRINCIPLES

LET GO OF WORRY
AND FEAR, LIVE IN
THE MOMENT.
LOVE LIFE.

Amanda Brown

First published in Great Britain by Practical Inspiration Publishing, 2019

The moral rights of the author have been asserted.

ISBN   9781788601368 (print)
       9781788601344 (mobi)
       9781788601351 (epub)

www.thelipstickprinciples.co.uk

Practical Inspiration
PUBLISHING

With love, appreciation and gratitude

To Mum and Dad, beautiful souls, for inspiring me, supporting me and loving me always.

To Jack Canfield for teaching me so much, and to all the many rock stars around the world I met through Jack.

To Lisa and Belinda for your unwavering support and confidence in my work.

To everyone I know who has stood up, stood out, shown up, fallen down and got back up again; you show me the way.

To all the leading ladies who have applied The LIPSTICK principles and changed their world; in doing so you have encouraged me to share more and write this book so everyone can apply their own LIPSTICK.

To Paul who has shown me love and allowed me to love from a place of no fear.

To all my wonderful friends and family, we all support each other in this world and together we achieve more.

> Some people come into your life for a reason
> Some for a season
> Some for a lifetime

Every person, every reason, every season I appreciate you.

I couldn't have done this without you guys and gals.

Love you x

CONTENTS

INTRODUCTION

I became a life coach over a decade ago and have worked with entrepreneurs, wildly successful business women and women who simply want to feel happy with their direction in life – women who want to feel in control, connected and with a sense of purpose. Over the last decade I've learnt, studied and practised a whole host of strategies and methodologies for feeling good and exploring how the mind works. In this book I'll share what has really worked for me and what's worked for other women to keep them sane and make them feel happy and in control.

The strategies work in different ways at different times. If you are flying high, they will help you fly higher. If you've lost your wings altogether, they'll help you find them and maintain a continuous feeling of control, direction and joy.

I've been dedicated for a long time to the idea that there is a process for feeling happy, letting go of worry and fear, and loving life. I began steadfastly sticking to certain routines and sharing them with others. Sometimes I was teaching and coaching these strategies when I wasn't necessarily feeling happy or successful myself. (Being a life coach doesn't necessarily mean you have it sorted to start with.) The results others achieved assured me the strategies worked, and even when times were s**t, I was committed to practising the ones which I now call the five a day (like eating your fruit and veg).

If you like the sound of not worrying or having self-doubt, and feeling like you can take the next step and achieve whatever you decide, then you are in the right place, and I hope to hold your hand through this book and lead you on the path to happiness and being in control of your life.

We need the strategies from *The LIPSTICK Principles* because life's not an easy ride. Sometimes we may be loving the wonderful ride of life and then bang, something happens, the ride has thrown us to the floor and it may feel as if we'll never get back on again. Every one of us at some point in our lives has felt lost, without a sense of direction, not good enough, emotional, stressed, rejected, out of control, fearful and wanting to give up and hide away, wishing that we could just wake up when everything was all sorted and life was back on track. (If you are the exception, do please drop me a note and say hi; I'd love to know how the heck you managed that.)

We all need something in these times to get us through, and these principles keep you rational, keep you calm and help you realise that this is just a moment in time. They also give you a structure and strategies to help you get clear on what you really want out of life and develop the confidence to make that happen.

If you've picked this book up or been gifted this book, it's in your hands for a reason. I hope through its contents you find strategies that make sense and stories that speak to your soul, and the reasons you were drawn to it or it was drawn to you become evident with every chapter.

This is a book that's full of personal stories on how the strategies and principles have worked for me. I've dedicated the last ten years to studying the strategies for being happy, and you cannot learn this stuff without applying it to your own life. I'll share examples of how the strategies have helped other women make decisions and achieve clarity on what they want, and how the strategies have changed the world of those who have applied them and the people close to them. With a little faith and a sprinkling of magic, they will make a difference to your world too. I don't want to put anyone off by mentioning magic. It isn't really about magic, it's about practising and applying daily disciplines – It just feels magical when you get the results.

The strategies are called the LIPSTICK principles, and they are a step-by-step guide to letting go of worry and fear, living in the moment and loving life. In this book you will learn how to apply the LIPSTICK principles in order to approach life from a place of love not fear. LIPSTICK is an acronym and each letter stands for a principle and is the subject of a chapter. Each chapter flows into the next, and the different strategies are all brought to life with stories that help make sense of how to apply that principle and when to use it.

Life Lessons – Learn the simple life lessons that put you in control of your life.

Imagine – Learn how to utilise your secret weapon, your mind, make decisions, review where you are now and use 'movies' to make decisions and create some meaningful goals for the future.

Presence – Learn how to be present with yourself and the people around you, how to still your mind and live in the moment.

Step In – Learn how to create momentum and how powerful the focus of just one step is to get you where you want to be.

Trust – Learn about universal energy and how to create the faith that everything will turn out just as you want. Believe that the universe is here to support you.

Invite Others In – Learn how to invite others in to help you get where you want to be and how to build a dream team of supporters. Plus how asking for help is the biggest strength you can have.

Confidence – Learn about super simple strategies to raise your self-esteem and harness the powerful connection between your body and mind to boost your confidence.

KISS (Keep It Simple Sweetheart) – Learn how to fill your love tank every day with the strategies that bring you joy, love and happiness; this is your five a day for a happy life.

The LIPSTICK principles teach you psychology-based strategies in a language which makes sense; they draw on a wide range of my training and study over the last ten years: including a master's in NLP (neurolinguistics programming, how the mind works), hypnosis, time line therapy (utilising past and future memories to create momentum and freedom in the present) and numerous successes and experiences in life coaching.

Behind the LIPSTICK principles there is one core guiding principle which knits them all together. This is to live life from a place of love not fear and say, 'I'm in.' This core guiding principle is very personal to me and has created a complete change in how I approach life and feel about the world around me, and how I feel about myself.

Before we get to each LIPSTICK principle in detail, I'd like to share a blog I wrote a while ago which led to me adopting the core principle to live my life from a place of *love not fear*. Throughout this book I'll share how this approach to life has changed my world and will change yours too. I was not completely aware I had adopted it until a few months after the worst thing that could happen in my world had actually happened. My lovely Mum passed away and this changed my approach to life in a most unexpected manner.

My first blog on living without fear

'I love you Mum and I couldn't do this without you...' This is a message I'd written in a card to Mum, my biggest supporter, a few short months before she passed away in 2017.

I meant every one of those words. I told Mum all the time what she and her support meant to me. I could never have imagined life without her. To me, losing Mum was the worst thing that could ever happen.

A few days after she died, I wrote her another card. This time the words were what I wanted her to hear wherever she was heading next. I told her again what she meant to me, how much I loved her and how I already missed her. I told her what she had taught me and how I had become who I am because of her guidance, love and support.

I also wrote: 'Mum, I always said I couldn't do this without you, and yet I'm still breathing, I'm still here, and so although I never thought it possible, the worst thing in my world has happened and I am still breathing, I am still here. Life is going to be different now but I'm functioning enough to help arrange the best send off for you, the guiding light in my life, and again I'm still breathing.'

The point is, when we imagine the unimaginable it terrifies us; we believe we won't be able to bear what we imagine. This is not simply about huge life-changing events like losing a loved one. We also imagine the worst in our everyday lives; we terrify ourselves with our thoughts about our work, our children, our friends or the world around us.

People asked me if losing Mum also brought me some good things, which in itself seemed a strange question. Initially, it confused me – how can something good come from the worst thing in the world?

Six months after Mum died, I realised something good had happened to me. I noticed I was no longer afraid. The worst thing had happened, and

I was still alive and still breathing. I even felt love around me and joy, joy in so many things.

In that moment I knew I had nothing to fear, and from that day forward I chose to lead life from a place of love and not fear.

I recognised the 12 learnings which led me to make this decision:

1. We will always survive, no matter how bad it seems at the time; we will continue to breathe and will cope and find a way through.
2. Everyone eventually adapts to change, and a new normal begins; no matter how big the change, everything will turn out OK in the end.
3. I have no control over anything, and every control over everything: I can plan my life and by creating goals I can make the most of my life and the precious time I have. Whilst I have no control over events such as death, illness, other people's actions, redundancy... I do have control over how I respond to every event in my life.
4. Emotions are completely natural and we want to experience them all. Emotions that make us feel deliriously happy or super sad are all a blessing. When we don't feel emotion, we aren't living. Life is not about creating a straight line with no ups or downs and no emotion; think about this – a straight line on a heart monitor means only one thing and that's

that life has ended. We want to have emotion; it means we are alive.

5. Kindness is the greatest gift and there will always be someone there in our hour of need if we reach out and let them in.

6. Small miracles can happen every day if we are open to seeing everything as a miracle: a phone call at just the right moment, a message on social media that seems to be perfectly timed, a rainbow in the sky or a white feather just as I am thinking of someone (I believe that signs like white feathers come from the universe).

7. Not everyone responds in the way we might imagine. How we expect someone to behave and what actually happens, in reality, can be polar distances apart. We cannot control other people and their responses, only the responses we have.

8. We are so much stronger than we can ever imagine.

9. There is no *right* way, only the way that we do it, and that's the best way we can.

10. It's OK not to be OK sometimes and this time will pass.

11. I am extremely grateful for everything and everyone in my life on a daily, hourly, moment-by-moment basis.

12. I have learnt to let things go, never to dwell on small things which really won't matter in a week's time. Getting caught up in small things

comes from fear and insecurity (see below for my biggest learn).

I learnt that I am not afraid: I didn't realise what that actually meant at first or even that I was feeling it. What it means to me is the worst thing in the world happened to me and I was OK, I was still breathing. *So, if the worst thing in the world that could happen to you has happened and you're OK, what have you got to be afraid of?*

This was the lesson I was deliriously happy to learn.

Knowing this means I'm able to 'play full out', in a manner I'm not really sure I had since being a kid.

Playing full out for me means greeting everyone with love and everything with anticipation and not being worried about or tied to the outcome. Ultimately, whatever happens in this wonderful life, everything will be OK eventually.

In effect, there are two ways you can approach life: from a place of joy and love or a place of fear. Fear-based living has us making decisions based on the fear of 'what if?'. What if I get hurt, what if it doesn't work out, what if it all goes wrong, what if I don't make it happen, what if I get rejected, what if something happens to them, what if... what if...?

Knowing I have no control over anything and full control over many things means I can choose to live life from a place of love not fear.

Everything will turn out just as it should: what if it *does work out*, what if it all *turns out perfectly*, what if I'm *welcomed*, what if I *do make it happen*?

Of course it will all turn out right in the end, because it does, and so long as I'm breathing I'm OK.

Fearless living doesn't mean jumping off cliffs or out of planes (unless that's what you want to do). Fearless living is opening your heart and soul to living life full out, connecting with souls just like you, and recognising that we are all here to make the most of the precious time we have, to make a difference to other people, to laugh, to love, to run if you want to run, to dance, to experience life in all its glory... to feel.

Mum had a little wooden sign at home that read as follows:

REACH FOR THE STARS
LIVE FOR EVERY MOMENT
DANCE LIKE NO ONE IS WATCHING
SING LIKE NO ONE IS LISTENING
LOVE LIKE THERE IS NO TOMORROW
FOLLOW YOUR DREAMS
LAUGH
CHOOSE WITH NO REGRET
SMILE UNCONDITIONALLY

(I would add to this: MAKE SOMEONE'S DAY and BE KIND.)

I've read that sign a hundred times and considered it a good way to think and live.

Six months after Mum passed away, when I experienced a feeling of joy again, I was actually feeling just like the sign said to and I was approaching life with an open heart.

My decisions were being made on the basis of 'what's the best that can happen?' rather than the worst. I was making decisions in the faith that even if the worst that could happen does happen, I would still be OK.

I realised I was living my life from a place of love not fear.

My Mum was a character and a very active woman. Whenever she was invited to do anything, be it body boarding in the sea, dancing, singing, climbing, walking, she would always say, 'Yes, I'M IN'... Then she would say, 'There may come a time when I can't do this', and she'd jump in.

The day came when Mum wasn't able to do it. I think of her every day, and through both her life and her death she has helped me learn to live a life filled with love and to not be afraid of anything.

When it comes to life, my new mantra is **'I'm in'**...
There is one thing guaranteed in the future, that
one day I won't be able to say this.

That was a blog post and every one of those lessons of 'letting go of fear' and 'letting love in' is threaded throughout this book, you will learn how to decide what you want on the basis of 'just go for it', 'say I'm in', 'connect with others and lead the life you know is possible'.

The purpose of this book is to share the LIPSTICK principles so you too can approach life from a place of love and experience consistent happiness within your life, not just in moments.

Lipstick itself as a make-up product is not new of course. It was created many years ago for the leading ladies of the silver screen to sparkle in front of the camera. We all play the leading lady in our own lives; some days we sparkle and some days we wish we had an understudy to stand in for us when we would rather hide behind the curtains.

The LIPSTICK principles are here to help every woman love life, step onto her own stage (this stage we call life), feel proud of her performance, write her own script and feel like she deserves a standing ovation every day. Happiness and success are not just for those who have been handed some magic wand; they are there for us all.

A few years ago I began speaking at large events and running training programmes. I developed exercises people could try in a room, and many of these exercises I share in the book – psychology-based success strategies made into a simple doable formula. The LIPSTICK principles are for women in the real world – women who have life thrown at them but who get back up and face it head on.

This *life manual* gives you all you need to step up, step out, go for promotions, ask for help, show love, be loved and feel great about where you are now and where you are heading next. I invite you to say, 'I'm in,' and let's start applying the LIPSTICK principles now.

LIFE LESSONS

Life from a place of love:

Life from a place of love means you can forgive more easily, let go of the past and have magnificent, open, loving relationships with people you already know and new people you meet. Feel positive and energised each day and attract similar people into your life. Feel proud of who you are and confident in your decisions; trust yourself and other people. Listen to your intuition and go with what feels right. Say yes to what you want and tell others what you want. Feel in control. Accept and respect others where they are in their lives. Be ready to take risks and step forward in a new direction. Love the experience of life. Create time for you and say yes to what you love. Feel full of love for you and your world.

Life from a place of fear:

Life from a place of fear is imagining the world is plotting against you, comparing yourself to others in a negative way, and feeling jealous of others' success. It is never wanting to share with others or allowing love in because of a fear of being hurt. It is talking yourself out of ideas, in case they don't work. It is looking at your life as sad or disappointing, or criticising yourself because of your position in life, weight, lack of money or anything else you can find to use against yourself. It is worrying about things that may never happen and complaining about situations that happen in your life.

Our first LIPSTICK principle is L for Life Lessons, and in this first principle you will learn about good fear and bad fear and how complaining can be really powerful in helping you understand what you really want. You will discover simple strategies that you can begin to implement immediately in order to feel in control of your decisions and how you spend your time. This principle gives you the insight and knowledge to say yes and no to what is right for you.

Firstly, I talk about coming from a place of love not fear throughout this book, although, just to clarify up front, some fear is really good for you. Good fear is when we feel nervous about doing something but go ahead and do it anyway, and something in us changes as a result of confronting that fear head on.

Good fear and bad fear

Good fear is that feeling when you are kind of excited about something but your first reaction to whatever it is is 'Ohhhhh, I don't know if I can do that', and doubt creeps in.

Twenty years ago, I decided it would be a good idea to jump out of a plane, so I volunteered for a 'tandem skydive' in New Zealand. My reason for doing this was that I wanted to feel braver. I had recently come out of a six-year relationship which hadn't done wonders for my confidence and I really wasn't sure what I was doing with my life. I had gone to visit my sister, who lives in New Zealand, to reflect on life.

I had this idea that doing something so out there would help me feel braver in life. I felt like life was changing around me, but I wasn't changing with life. When you come out of a relationship, whether voluntarily or after being 'dumped', there is a holding period when you know the future you had been thinking about isn't happening any more, but you haven't created a new future yet. And if your confidence has been knocked, it can be hard to start thinking about what the new future looks like. Similarly, if you've ever been made redundant or experienced a situation which inadvertently changes the course you thought you were on, you know that the direction isn't the same any more but you haven't quite caught up with life events to decide what the new next is. I felt a bit stuck, so I thought doing something terrifying could unstick me and help me feel braver about facing the new next.

So, I did it, I jumped... (When I say jumped, I mean I sat on the edge of the plane and my instructor peeled my hands away from the door, and with her weight

behind me we gracefully fell out of the plane.) Scary –
yes, fear – yes, but good fear!

When I reached the ground in one piece, I kind of
skipped and floated across the ground to the car park
and instantly knew something had changed in me.
I felt lighter, and I did actually feel braver. Within a
few days I noticed I began talking to my sister about
things I'd like to do in the future. It had worked...
experiencing good fear had helped me see I could look
forward again.

I do talks on love and fear and often in my seminars
I'll ask the audience this question: what would you do
if you had no fear? Without fail at least two or three
people in the audience will say that if they had no fear,
they would jump out of a plane. I talk to them about
what a skydive could do for them, how they could feel,
how this could change how they approach life in the
future. Yet even though they would like to and they
hear it could be a fantastic experience, they do not do
it. Because of fear.

Other answers come up like quit my job and travel the
world, retrain in a new career, find love, run a marathon,
do stand-up comedy, start a business... These are all
life-changing events which people would do if they
had no fear, but they do have fear, and this fear, the
fear that stops you doing things you really want to do,
is not good fear. It's bad fear. It's fear controlling you

and what you could be, do or have in life if you didn't have the bad fear. When I talk of fear throughout the book, it's the bad fear that I am referring to.

Good fear, which pushes you outside your comfort zone, can be a gift; it shows up as nerves to remind us we're doing something for the first time. Jumping out of a plane may be an extreme way to test the nerves, but making changes in your life that may make you nervous will build confidence and build your resilience to fear.

Think for a moment. When you get nervous, where do you experience the nerves? By that I mean: do you get nerves in your tummy like butterflies? Or perhaps across your shoulders? There will be a place in your body where you feel nerves. Think back to the last time you experienced nerves and notice where you were feeling them. For me, nerves appear in my tummy; that's where I experience nervousness. Coincidentally, when I experience excitement it's also in my tummy and often, weirdly, across my shoulders.

Think of the last time you felt excitement; where was the feeling for you? Are excitement and nerves both felt in similar places? If, as in my case, they are, you will see that maybe nerves and excitement can be interchanged, so when you look at good fear you can think about it as exciting nerves. Nerves are good, and there is good fear and bad fear.

You are in control

When I wrote the blog on the 12 lessons I learnt about living without fear, point number three was this:

> I have learnt I have no control over anything, and full control over everything.

Sounds confusing? Let's look at control. Here is a list of things over which we have little or no control:

- the weather
- death
- accidents
- illness (some control if preventative)
- tragic events that happen in the world
- other people's reactions or actions

On the flip side, although the above list seems long, the great news is that we do have control over everything else – or rather we have full control over ourselves. We have control over what happens in our world, and we have control over our responses to what happens in the wider world. We can choose what we do, where we go, what we think, how we feel and how we fill our time.

This is a very good thing to know; we have control over many things, and so we can lead our life based on choices we make. We can choose to lead our life by choice (not chance).

Cathartic complaining

As women we are renowned for putting others' needs ahead of our own, and for not being clear on what we really want. We rarely complain. Yes, we may have a bit of a moment with friends, talking/complaining about work or our partner or how we have put on a few pounds, or how busy we are, but we are talking to friends so it's not really moaning or complaining; it is most definitely bonding! But we do and can complain about some interesting things.

In the UK we openly moan and complain about the weirdest things. We complain about the weather – over which we have no control. Perhaps, like me, you've occasionally done a little call out to the sunshine fairies: 'Please, please let it shine this weekend.' We complain about how negative the news is – we can't control the news. I was an avid fan of *GMTV* and *Good Morning Britain*; I grew up with Lorraine Kelly at my breakfast table and I loved her light-hearted empathetic approach to people. It was like watching a glossy magazine. I used to say *GMTV* and Lorraine were my window to the world, as this was pretty much the only news I watched. When Piers Morgan started on *Good Morning Britain* with his strong views and big debates, it felt like I was watching a battle at breakfast each day and I moaned about that. Of course I (like everyone else) have no control over Piers Morgan or how a TV show changes its format. I did of course eventually realise I had control over which channel I watched.

Traffic, there's a big one. We can spend quite a lot of time complaining about travel and traffic, over which we have very little or no control.

So why is it so easy to complain and moan about the things over which we have no control? Well, it's precisely because we have no control over them, so we can complain because we don't have to do anything about them. But when we complain about our jobs, the way someone treats us, our weight, our lack of money, the amount we drink, feeling unhappy, feeling low on self-esteem, not being fit... we know deep down we actually have control over these things and we just might have to do something about them.

I want you to complain. I want you to moan and complain, and complain some more, about any of the parts of your life you feel like complaining about. Have a 'complainathon' and get it all out, from a place of love, because:

a. it's cathartic, and
b. if we're complaining, it means something big

It means, deep down somewhere, we know there is something different out there for us, something better, something much better.

We only really complain because we have some kind of reference deep inside that there is something different, something better than what we have right now. If we complain about the quality of food or service in a restaurant, it's because we have experience of better food or better service. If we complain about the price of holidays at half-term or the price of petrol on a motorway, we know (or believe) that it's being offered cheaper elsewhere. If we complain about our boss being hard work, we've heard of or had experience of a great boss. If we complain about our weight, we have at some time in the past known what a different weight feels like. If our partners don't pay us enough attention or help us at home, we've seen or experienced other partners who do. If we complain about the hours we work, we know there are other people who don't work the long hours we do. If we complain about the way our life is right now, we have an idea that life could be better.

Complaining + Inspiration = Opportunity

Complaining is cool. Complaining can really be one of the first steps to deciding what we want. Complaining must mean that we know what we *don't* want, and if we know what we *don't* want, it's only a hop, skip and a jump to getting clarity on what we *do* want. Complaining plus a sprinkle of inspiration is our opportunity to decide what better looks like for us.

Being in conscious control (and accepting that control) means we can make choices. We can decide what we accept, what we do, when we do it, how we do it and, of course, the implications *if we did it*.

Choosing not to create change is still a choice.

Ultimately, if we want something to change, we'll have to make a change, which could be scary; it could be exciting but, more likely, a little scary to start with, but it won't remain scary for long. The scary part can be thinking about it and that's the bit that can take time, but something in us will alert us to the fact that it's time for change and then it's our choice.

In the last couple of years I've been going through the menopause and a few months ago I noticed my body shape changing. I've always been about the same shape and weight but suddenly things looked different – my body was becoming 'larger and looser'... I groaned a bit and came up with some reasonable explanations (excuses): maybe it's because I'm so happy that my whole body has relaxed! However, all I know for sure is that, seemingly overnight, I'm about a stone heavier than I've ever been. I looked up 'menopause' online and read that when women go through menopause, the composition of their body changes and the muscle starts to turn to fat. Having always done the same amount of exercise and eaten the same amount, this jolly fact online told me I will not get the same results from continuing to do the same thing – the exercise and diet I'm used to are not going to cut it any more. I'm in a place where to get a different result, I'll have to do something differently.

I have three choices:

1. Complain about the menopause and generally being a woman (done a bit of that and it didn't change anything).
2. Accept it and replace my whole wardrobe (expensive).
3. Change my diet and exercise routine.

Complaining from a place of love + INSPIRATION = Being in control and opportunity
Complaining from a place of fear = I have no control, I am powerless

Sadly, many would rather continue to complain, rendering them powerless in situations they could take control of and change. They may complain for the rest of their lives about things over which they have full control and they choose not to do anything to change their circumstances. This is a shame because we are the lucky ones – we do have the choice. It's worse still when people stop complaining altogether; at this stage they have surrendered to a situation they have the power to change.

The Serenity Prayer
God grant me the serenity to accept the things
I cannot change,
Courage to change the things I can
And the wisdom to know the difference

Choosing not to do something is still a choice – maybe not as conscious a choice as making a change but it's still a choice.

Exercise

This is an exercise designed to help you recognise the things in life that you complain about or would like to change and establish which ones you have control over. Then you can decide what you would like instead; it's a step towards working out what you really want and feeling in control of your life.

On the left-hand side of a sheet of paper (see the layout opposite), jot down anything you have complained about in the last week, either to yourself or openly to others. Add anything from the weather to the car needing cleaning, your job, wardrobe or energy levels. This list can be as long as you like; add new complaints to it when you catch yourself thinking or saying them.

Once you have completed the list, look at each complaint or thing you would like to change and in the middle column just mark down whether you believe it's something in your control or not (with a yes or a no). If it is not in your control, write this: 'I let this go, it is not in my control.' If you find yourself fixating on things that are out of your control, just repeat the sentence every time: 'I let this go, it is not in my control.'

Complaints or things you want to change	Is this in your control, yes or no?	What do you want instead? ('I want ....')

Now you have a list of things that are in your control; next to each of these think about what the complaint is, why it's a complaint and what it is you want instead. Remember we will only really complain about something because we have a reference of something better.

Here are some examples. If you caught yourself saying the car is dirty, then on the opposite side of the paper write: 'I want a clean car.' If you have complained about being tired recently, on the opposite side of the paper write: 'I want to have energy.' If you complained about working late, write: 'I want to finish work on time.' Write the statement in the last column as a positive statement which starts with the words 'I want'; this is important, as it needs to be written as a want not a don't want. So, 'The car is dirty' has to become 'I want a clean car' not 'I don't want a dirty car'. Saying the words 'don't want' is talking in what is known as 'away from' language, which means you are still using words which describe what you don't want in this case ('dirty car' still appears in the sentence). Your statement needs to be a 'towards' statement, something you want ('clean car' needs to appear in the sentence).

You will end up with a list of things you want, not a list of things you don't want, and this will come in handy later in the book when we move further into deciding what you really want and taking control of your life.

A life of choice not chance

A life of choice and taking control is a conscious commitment to back yourself; it is saying: 'I've got this, I can do it *if* I want to.' A life of chance is leaving our outcomes to other people or fate, and it doesn't need to be that way. Realising we are in full control gives us choices and we can choose in favour of what we want, not what others want.

Wherever we are right now in life, it is because of choices we have made in the past. A friend shared with me that when she was just 23, she decided to save 10% of her salary every month without fail. As her salary rose, so did her contribution. At the age of 48 she has a savings account with over a quarter of a million pounds in it despite being paid a very average wage in the NHS. What a fabulous choice to make; I wish I'd made a similar choice at her age! I didn't. I chose to spend not save. Can I remember now what I spent that 10% on? Of course not.

When I bought my first house, I remember putting little piles of things that needed to go upstairs on the bottom step, something I used to do when I lived at home. After I'd gone upstairs a few times and hadn't taken the things up (like Mum used to do), it dawned on me: 'Oh… that will be my job then to take them up – there is no one else going to do it for me. If it's meant to be, it's up to me – I'm in charge here.'

The simple fact is, if we want something to be different, we must do something differently. But it's not always easy, is it? It can take a long time to realise you can change what isn't working for you. For Kara it took a health scare to really see that things needed to change.

I had known Kara a long time and she was always full of energy; she had time for everyone, loved her job and was really good at it. She was head of design for a large organisation and travelled a couple of times a year to the Far East and America in her role, as well as commuting to work each day, which took a minimum of 90 minutes. Her job always seemed so exciting and really rewarding to her, and her husband also worked long hours and loved his job.

Kara then had her daughter and became a Mum and things changed. Firstly, the ninety-minute commute meant her daughter was in a nursery for long days, and then there was the gauntlet she ran with the motorway each day, often getting stuck and feeling anxious she wouldn't get back in time to pick her daughter up. Kara was leaving the house at 6.30 a.m. and getting back at 6.30 p.m. four days a week. The long trips to the Far East which once felt exciting became a wrench to Kara, as she would have to leave her daughter for a week at a time. While she was off on maternity leave, the management team at work had changed, and the boss she got along with really well had left. To Kara the whole landscape had changed and she had more responsibility and less time. She used to not mind working at home in the evening sometimes, but now with a little girl to spend time with this wasn't really an option; if she did work at home, it would be late at night, and she began to get exhausted.

We often met on Friday evenings for a catch-up and Kara started cancelling these catch-ups, saying she was literally falling asleep on the sofa at 8 p.m. Texts would go unanswered and when I saw Kara she looked exhausted and pale. When I spoke to her she was always tired, and we often discussed her situation and chatted about changing it. But it was hard. This was the role Kara had worked her whole life for; the job was part of her. She loved design and she knew that in the area where she lived there would be no opportunities to do this. She was also an independent woman, always worked hard and had her own income.

Kara being tired most nights was not doing anything for her relationship either; her husband worked late in his job and Kara was often already asleep when he got home. We would have continual conversations around her changing her role or circumstances, and Kara would say, 'I can't, I can't, what would I do?' All her friends wanted to help; it was sad to see someone with so much spark start to fizzle out. Kara even got to the stage where she said, 'I'm not even going to complain about this any more, I'm sick of hearing myself complain and not do anything about it.'

Realising how little energy she had, she visited an acupuncturist who told her her body was exhausted, and if she didn't change something she would become ill. Even with this information she still found it tough; she didn't know what she would do, or how she would do it, but eventually, after nearly a year of being exhausted and trying to do everything, she finally made the decision that it was time to change. She stopped saying 'I can't' for the first time and started thinking 'I can and I will'.

She made quite a radical change in the end, moving to a job with far less responsibility, three days a week and close to home. Almost immediately you could see the difference, just from not having to spend three hours a day in the car just to get to and from work. Kara had time again for her friends and was able to do fitness again. Ultimately, though it took time, Kara said yes to her health and her family and no to the big job. About six weeks after leaving that job she looked like a different person, as if life had been pumped back into her. Her spark was back and she said she felt as though she had been half dead for the last year, but now she could feel life and energy flowing through her body again.

Saying no to a big salary is a huge step-change for any woman, and yet ultimately time and health are the most valuable things any of us have, and Kara chose to spend her valuable time with her family.

When we think we can't change something, we feel stuck, we get tired, and it's hard to think when we're exhausted. The more we say, 'I can't,' the less control we feel we have and it renders us powerless. Imagine if we simply used the word 'won't' instead of 'can't'. 'I won't change things' at least recognises our personal responsibility for the decision!

Yes and no buzzers

A really simple strategy for feeling in control of your time, your decisions and your life is to begin utilising the yes and no buzzers. Imagine for a moment that in front of you are two large buzzers; buzzer one has the word 'Yes' on it, and buzzer two has the word 'No'. When I imagine mine, the yes buzzer is green and the no buzzer is red. (I don't actually have to imagine these buzzers any longer, as a kind client actually bought me a set of buzzers as a gift!)

Now you can picture the buzzers in front of you, I want to explain how they work as it's a super simple strategy that puts you in control of your life. The thing you need to know: your buzzers are working constantly all day long, whether you are operating them purposefully or not. Think of Kara sitting on the motorway every day; she was constantly saying yes to her work and no to time with her family and to her health. Even though she felt she had no choice, she did have the choice. Kara knew that; remember she actually said, 'I know I'm choosing this so I won't complain any more.' For nearly a year she was saying no to creating change and yes to having things stay the same.

Taking control of your life is the time for you to say yes to you. To say yes to you involves deciding what you really want. Everything is a choice: working late or going on a date, looking for a new job or sticking with a job you don't love, eating healthily or eating badly, the glass of wine or the glass of water.

I was on a short internal flight in the UK last year with only a handful of passengers in a small plane. There were just two seats either side of the aisle. A member of cabin crew approached two women at the front of the plane and explained that, as they were sitting next to the exit (often a favoured seat since it offers extra leg room), should there be a problem while we were in the air, they would be responsible for opening the emergency exit door. The woman who was sitting closest to the exit was around 25 and, rather than watch the demonstration the air hostess was about to give, she did something unexpected. She said, 'Oh, I'd rather not take on that responsibility.' A chap sitting behind her immediately said he would swap seats. I thought it was pretty cool that this young woman was assured enough to say no to the responsibility, as it likely meant she was saying yes to relaxing on the flight rather than feeling nervous the whole time.

When you're working and see a friend's number come up on your phone in the middle of the day, you decide in that moment whether you want to say yes to a half-hour chat and no to finishing the work. Or perhaps you are with a friend and another friend calls: are you saying yes to the friend you're sitting in front of and no to the caller, or yes to the caller and no to giving the person you are with your full attention?

How often do you not get round to doing something you want to because time has flown by, or because you've allowed someone or something else to take your time? I hear about more and more people who are office based working one day a week from home because they can get more done with no interruptions. It's tough when you work in an office and people pop over and ask if you have five minutes; in that moment you operate your yes or no buzzer. You may say yes to giving them five minutes (which usually turns into 20) as it feels good to help people. However, in that moment we need to recognise that we are saying no to getting our stuff done. It is a choice, and making it consciously and assertively is what puts us in control.

If you are clear about what you want, that makes the operation of your buzzers much easier. Success flows for those who learn to say no.

Time is our most valuable asset

Time is the most valuable thing each of us has to spend. The best bank account we all hold, and all have in common, is our bank account of time. We receive 24 shiny new hours into our accounts every evening at midnight. We hopefully sleep through the first six or seven and then, after that, it's up to us what we do with those hours, minutes, seconds.

The buzzers are being pressed all day long, regardless of whether we are aware that we are pressing them or not; the part that puts us in full control is becoming acutely aware of what we want and knowing that we operate our yes and no buttons. There is no right or wrong here. Whatever you choose to do with your time is fine; it's actually knowing that it's your choice that leads to you feeling in control.

Sometimes we say yes to others because we love helping people, and so we gain, even though we may say no to something else we were going to do for ourselves with our time. We might say yes to a couple of extra drinks on a night out in the knowledge that we are saying no to feeling fresh the next morning; it's all good, it is our choice. We are choosing to do this.

We may stay in jobs for a short while that don't feel great because we get paid well, and at that stage we say yes to saving and no to feeling great at work. We may say no to acting on an idea or changing things or going for what we want, because we don't know how to make it happen. My hope is that, with this book and all you learn through the LIPSTICK principles, you choose to operate your yes buzzer to going for it and no buzzer to potential regret. My hope is that you say no to fear and yes to love and what you really want.

Have you ever been in a relationship or job which doesn't feel quite right? Maybe that's where you are right now? Relationships that are not quite right are tough for a number of reasons. There are so many questions and quandaries to face. When you're in a relationship that doesn't feel quite right, chances are you spend a lot of time questioning two things:

1. yourself
2. your partner

If the basic fact is that you really want to be in a relationship, then there is so much of you that says yes to the relationship. However, when it isn't quite working, you may also be saying no to feeling really happy. The questions start in your mind: is it me, is there something wrong with me? Or is it them, they are not the one, it's their fault. It always feels like there should be someone to blame in relationships and criticism either of ourselves or of our partner kicks in. Neither strategy works well, and all this soul searching and quandary can lead to low self-esteem, especially when you're wondering if it's you. We might complain to a friend or to our partner; but all we really want is a great relationship and to give and receive love.

If we consider saying no to the relationship, we might imagine that life will be wonderful afterwards – we'll find our soul mate and all will be well – but the fear kicks in and our mind might go to the fear of never finding anyone and being alone for the rest of our lives (big-fear thoughts coming through).

Any of this sound familiar? The fact is that some relationships just don't work; it's sad but true. We can spend years deciding whose fault it is and trying to make it work, not wanting to give up, like Kara in her job. I have been there and now I've created a mantra in life for any situation that is causing so much angst and indecision:

If it's not a HELL YES, it's a NO.

Clients have used this mantra to turn down work, say no to dates, say no to holidays, and to say yes to clients, yes to new hobbies If it's not a hell yes, it's a no, and if it's a hell yes, then it's yes, yes, yes.

It's only when we have the courage to operate those buzzers and say no to some things that are just not working or doing it for us that we can say yes to others and let new things in.

Summary of the L of the LIPSTICK principles – Life Lessons

- Good fear and nerves are good for you; when you do something that you feel nervous about, you have changed something in you forever, you have shown yourself you're brave and you can do it. Embrace the nerves; in time they will become excitement.
- Start your 'complainathon' and write down all your complaints; add a little inspiration and

decide what you would like instead. If this is something in your control, it's time to 'feel the nerves' and change.

- You have no control over many things and every control over many things.
- Time is your most valuable asset; choose how you spend it and spend it in favour of yourself.
- You are in control of your yes and no buzzers; spend a day noticing what you are saying yes to and what you are saying no to, and start saying yes to what you want.
- New mantra in life: 'If it's not a HELL YES, it's a NO!'

LIPSTICK PRINCIPLE 2

IMAGINE

Imagine from a place of love:

Have you ever daydreamed about a holiday or pictured yourself lying on a beach with the sun shining down on you, laughing and having a fantastic time? It makes you feel good, doesn't it? Perhaps you have planned a big event, a wedding or a birthday party, and visualised everyone there having a great time and everything going smoothly. This is using your imagination from a place of love, everything going perfectly and turning out just as you planned. With this picture in your mind you don't experience nerves or fear, because your imagination has created a beautiful image full of love; the event hasn't happened and yet you can feel it, see it and almost experience it. You can imagine how you feel at the event, and you are genuinely excited. Imagining from a place of love is utilising images to create a future you want to move towards, and you feel excited about what lies ahead for you, because you have created some goals and decided what you want in the future.

Imagine from a place of fear (fantasy fear):

> Imagine from a place of fear is not making decisions on what you would really like in your life, and not having goals that excite you. It is feeling nervous about saying what you really want because you find it hard to think that it's possible. It's thinking about future events with a head full of worry and letting these thoughts make you feel anxious and dreading the future. It's not making decisions (being stuck in indecision) or feeling you have no choice over what life can be like. It's not letting yourself dream about the future and leaving life to chance.

In our next LIPSTICK principle, I for Imagine, you will learn how your thoughts and the images you use are your most powerful and secret weapon for feeling excited about the future and creating the life you want. This Imagine chapter explains why deciding what you want and creating goals are part of being in control and leading your life from a place of choice not chance. You will learn how being a movie maker helps you let go of worry and fear.

To start with, I want to share something really important with you: *your mind doesn't actually distinguish between something real and something imagined, at least in terms of the emotional response the idea or the event generates.* That's why you can experience feelings of fear and anxiousness about future events or pure excitement, with butterflies in your stomach, just by imagining that future event.

Your mind, like most secret weapons, needs to be trained in how it can be used safely and effectively to get the results you want. You're about to become a professional at having thoughts which create inspiring and empowering images and movies which light you up. You're about to crack the code for feeling good and excited about your future, and letting go of worry and fear.

When I see anyone who is experiencing anxiety or worry about the future, it's because they are running a horror movie of their own life. I don't know about you, but I personally don't like horror movies; I'm not even a fan of a thriller. I really feel the suspense and get jumpy when I know a drama or thriller has the potential to scare me. The solution is easy: I just don't watch them. I say no to feeling tense when it comes to that genre of movies. I also rarely watch the news these days; it's just too much negativity for me just before bed.

The great thing is that we are in control of what we watch on the box, and what media we consume on our phones; we are in control of this and more importantly (and this is the biggy) we have control over the movies we create in our own mind. These mind movies are the ones where we really want to get hold of the remote control! Coming from a place of love and not fear, you will be able to stop and pause any movies which create fear and write your own happy ending.

Use your mind to make the right movies

Becoming trained in creating the right movies in your mind is a skill that requires some practice, but the rewards are incredible, as you let go of fear, step into love and start creating the movies that excite you.

Note: You may or may not be aware that you run movies in your mind; it may feel more like a succession of thoughts that lead to a feeling or emotion. Some people see images much more naturally or are aware of them more than others.

When I was first introduced to the concept of visualising or creating mind movies, I was studying my master's in NLP and I hadn't really heard of visualisation. Curious about the concept, I turned to friends and asked the question, 'Do you visualise?' I was honestly surprised when friends immediately said yes and went on to share when they did it and what for.

Vanessa, who is super creative and has an incredible home, in terms of both the design and decoration, immediately told me how she often lies in bed in the evening and in her mind imagines redecorating rooms in her home; she tries out different colours and styles until she decides on the right one. What a great concept for mind movies, and I had no idea she used this powerful strategy!

Cherryl, whom I had always admired for how many plates she juggles without dropping any, shared that she lies in bed in the evening and imagines that she is an air-traffic controller in an airport. She visualises all the tasks she has to do the next day as planes all asking for permission to land. For each task she either assigns it a time to land or sends it back off around the world to request permission to land tomorrow. Wow, what an incredible way of using movies to organise time and tasks! (I would never have known what my friends did with visualisation; I was oblivious.)

It's years later now, and I know that visualising and movie making is the secret weapon to enhancing so much of our future. Don't worry if you haven't done it before; I hadn't either until I was first introduced to it. It's also fine if you feel you create movies more verbally as a chain of thoughts rather than full-blown movies and images. Thoughts without the images are just as powerful; it's the practice of thinking, visualising or making a movie of the future which creates the change for you.

The movies which make us anxious, upset or fearful often start with us having thoughts about the future turning out badly. They usually start with two words, 'what if', and then generally move quite rapidly into a downward spiral of negative endings. What if it all goes wrong? What if they don't like me? What if I don't get it? And so it goes on, with more and more what ifs.

I have changed these two words into one, changed 'what ifs' to 'WHIFs', and we all know what we do with WHIFs (bad smells): we wave our hand in front of our nose and move away from them as quickly as possible. That's exactly what I want you to be able to do.

Here are some common WHIFs that lead to people feeling anxious or worrying (experiencing bad fear): What if I mess up the interview? What if they meet someone else? What if I don't get the house, the job, the money? What if the party isn't a success? What if I can't do it? What if I fail? What if they get ill? What if they die? What if I don't pass? What if they go off me? What if the business goes under? What if I get found out? What if I don't get the promotion? What if I look stupid? They go on and on. Choose whichever WHIF resonates with you; I'm sure there is one.

To let go of worry and fear, live in the moment and feel happy in life; we have to get used to losing the negative what ifs and flipping them round, from 'what if it all goes wrong?' to 'what if it all goes right?'.

What happens in your mind is that when you think of a fear-based what if, your mind begins creating a movie (or thoughts) of the event playing out, and this triggers a horrible negative feeling and emotion in you. Before you know it, you have spiralled to a bad place; that place doesn't yet exist in the future but it feels s**t!

The good news is that these events haven't happened yet and so you don't have to feel this way. All you need to learn to do is run a different movie, a movie based on 'what if it all goes right?'. When you can take control of the thoughts and movies, you can take control of the feelings and to a certain extent of the future.

Imagine if all the thoughts and movies that played in your head were about great things happening in the future – no disasters, just great things. To become your own blockbuster happy movie maker, it just takes a little practice.

The moment you know you are using your imagination to create anxiety and fear, you notice a negative feeling, sinking in the tummy or worry, and then you can use that same powerful imagination to say stop, rewind and run a similar movie with a happy ending. Say no to fear and yes to love.

Here is an example of a method I use for using mind movies to help people who are stuck in indecision and fear, and worrying about the future, to gain clarity on what they really want and lose the fear. This example is related to Lou, who was unhappy in her marriage, but the same technique can be used if you've been trying to decide whether it's time for a change in any area of your life. It's for changing any circumstances in which you don't feel quite right just now and will help you decide if you should take the leap or stick with the status quo.

Lou was married and having a horrendous time in her marriage. She had struggled for a number of years and had regularly tried changing things at home to improve the situation. But nothing did change. She was being worn down by the effort to try to make it work, while her husband did nothing. She was upset a lot of the time, either sad about how bad it had got or angry at him for not trying. It was crunch time; she knew she had to either accept the situation for what it was and say yes to staying married or leave the marriage and say no to feeling unhappy and dissatisfied on a regular basis. She had tried everything else to make it better.

But she was scared… there were a lot of WHIF's. What if she felt worse outside of the marriage? What if she was going to be on her own for ever? What if she regretted it? Those what ifs are normal; it's quite natural to fear the unknown.

To help her get unstuck and find some clarity with this situation, I invited her to create some mental movies of the future. First, I asked Lou to imagine for a moment that she and her husband separated today. Right now. Then, for the purpose of the movie, I asked her to project forward, one year ahead. The dust had settled and she was OK and he was OK. Against that backdrop, I asked her to imagine what might be happening in her life.

'Oh,' she said, and her face lit up, 'if it's one year from now I could have started dating again. In fact, yes I have started dating again, and it's my weekend without the kids. The guy I've just started dating has invited me to the Lakes and we are climbing a mountain. We are sitting on top of the mountain, drinking from a flask, and I'm really happy. I feel hope about the future and it's so good to meet someone who loves hiking like I do. It feels great.' I could see how good she felt because she was glowing just *imagining* it.

Next I said, 'OK, so clear that image for a moment and imagine now that it's one year from today and nothing has changed. You're still with your husband and the situation hasn't changed at all from how it's been for the last couple of years.' Immediately her body language changed, she slumped, and the colour drained from her. I could tell she was really seeing it and feeling it. She said, 'Oh, it's awful, it's got worse, I can't stand it.'

In that moment she knew she had a choice and she knew which choice she was going to make. Although she had been scared of making a change, in fact the bigger fear, the scariest thing, the reality came when she thought about how life would be if things stayed the same.

That image of her sitting on top of a mountain, drinking from a flask, feeling happy, was the image she kept in her mind when she had to endure the toughest part of making change: actually taking the first step and doing it. It's so important that you have a 'why' when making change, a place you want to be as opposed to where you currently are – an image of somewhere you want to be that compels you to be brave and create change.

Just over a year later a mutual connection of Lou's and mine was getting married in the Lake District. We agreed to travel together to the wedding. In the car on the way, Lou shared with me that she would be staying in the Lakes for an additional day following the wedding, because the guy she had recently started seeing was going to join her and they were going to walk up a mountain together! How cool is that. The exact image she had created to get her unstuck was actually now the reality, and one year on the dust had settled, and everyone was OK. That is the power of your imagination, when you use it to think about what you want (not what you don't).

Big decisions are scary. But when you come to them from a place of love and imagine everything working out brilliantly, then you can have the strength to see things through. Was Lou scared about making the change? Yes, of course. She worried about the impact on everyone of the decision she made. But the fear that nothing would change at all was stronger than the fear of making the change. She knew the change she decided on gave her a chance of something better.

Exercise

Think of a situation you are stuck in indecision over and fast forward a year. If you have made no change at all, what does the future look and feel like? If you take the leap and make the change (and all goes well), what does the future look and feel like one year from now?

If we allow fear to rule our decisions, our world becomes smaller and we begin shrinking within it. I want women to step into a place of love and trust in the future, and to have the confidence to create change and lead a life that's right for them.

You can practise making positive mini-movies about all areas of your life. Lie in bed in the morning and play through the day ahead with everything going perfectly; picture the day as a movie just as you want it to play out, with all outcomes positive. Notice how great it feels.

If there is a situation coming up that makes you feel nervous, practise running that situation through where everything turns out just as you would want. Practise the good movies and you will see nerves disappear very soon. It's impossible to feel nervous about something that works out perfectly!

Here's a quick summary:

- Your mind doesn't know the difference between reality and imagination, but it will create emotions to reflect what you are thinking.
- Use your mind to think of a movie where anything you are nervous about works out just as you wanted it to.
- If you are stuck in indecision, fast forward a year and imagine two scenarios, one for each decision, and see which feels best and go with that (your decision and bravery will appear). Sometimes the idea of nothing changing is worse than the thought of it changing.
- New mantra: 'I only make movies with happy endings.'

Goals and wants

Now let's move on to the most important thing: deciding what you want.

When I was little, I used to say 'I want' for things I wanted and, in reply, I used to hear the words 'I want never gets'. A loving term used, I'm sure, to stop me nagging for things or perhaps to encourage me to use better language, such as 'Please can I have?'. It even got used almost like a melody whenever one of us kids said 'I want'; we would all turn round as a family and say, 'I want never gets.'

Ten years ago I started my first studies into how we humans work, how our minds are wired and what can help to make us happy. It was during this training that I learnt about how what we *say* to ourselves creates our *reality*. So, for me, the fact that every time I heard the words 'I want', I'd immediately hear in my head the childhood melody of 'I want never gets', meant that I really wasn't good at asking for things or being clear about what I really wanted.

Writing goals was all new to me, I had never really given any thought to why some people achieved so much and others not. I'd always been a very impulsive person rather than a planner or a big dreamer.

I also discovered at that stage that if I wanted to get better at creating goals and thinking about what I wanted in the future, I would need to rewrite the life script of 'I want never gets' and come up with a new melody: 'if you don't want, you won't get!'

During that period of training I created my first ever written goals, a list of things I'd love to happen in the next five years. I wanted to be running a business coaching and helping others reach their potential; I wanted to travel with my work and continue to study; I wanted to be fit enough to run a 10k, and I wanted to feel healthy and enjoy holidays.

Rob was someone I met during this training and we worked on our five-year visions together. His vision felt bigger and more specific than mine. He said in five years' time he would be living in Los Angeles, working as a consultant and have a dog called Dexter.

To make the goals stronger we learnt the art of creating mind movies of where we would be in five years, reflecting on what we had achieved. I teach this method now, and how you do it is to imagine it's a time in the future (in this case five years) and you have achieved everything you set out to achieve. Create an image of where you will be sitting and what you will be feeling, and add as much detail as you can to that future image. I imagined that I would be sitting in the sunshine, feeling happy and proud of what I had achieved (with a glass of wine in hand). Rob and I stayed in contact for a while and I visited him in London a couple of times, and then we lost touch.

In 2014, I was continuing my studies into personal transformation and had flown over to the US for training with Jack Canfield, who is an incredible trainer and coach, co-author of *The Chicken Soup for the Soul* series and *The Success Principles*. I went out a couple of days ahead of the programme with a friend and enjoyed a sunny Sunday exploring Santa Monica and Venice beach. We had chosen a bar at Venice beach to refresh ourselves with a glass of wine. The beer garden was hot and opened directly onto the boardwalk.

As I sat in the sunshine, I was thinking how lucky I was to be here embarking on another new adventure and reflecting on the last five years as a coach; I also thought of the people I'd worked with, the fun I'd had and how exciting it was to be here in a different country studying and growing. I closed my eyes and felt the warmth of the sun on my face and had... a moment. One of those moments when you feel a little overwhelmed by where you are and where you have come from. Savoring the moment with my eyes closed I felt a shadow across my face and thought a cloud must have passed over the sun. I opened my eyes; it wasn't a cloud, it was a person standing directly in front of me. I couldn't see their face at first, but they said my name, 'Amanda'. Who did I know in LA? As they moved out of the sun, I saw them – it was Rob! He had moved to LA a couple of years before and was out walking his dog, Dexter!

It was close to five years since we had both written out our vision of where we would like to be in five years, and here we were brought together to remember and celebrate!

Deciding what you want

Is it easy to start thinking about what you really want in your life and setting goals? If we've left life to chance not choice in the past, it may be a new experience to decide what you really want and create goals for the future. It is this action of creating goals that makes us excited about the future and love life.

I use the analogy of a shopping list to show why writing a list of what you really want to do, be or have is a great idea. You have created a big shopping list at home, full of everything you want for the week ahead and to stock your cupboards. Off you set to the supermarket and when you arrive, you suddenly realise your shopping list is on the counter top at home. You know that feeling! Since you wrote it, you've done a million things and you have to try to recall what you wanted!

We could walk into the shop with the thought, 'I'll just take anything and go home with bags full of items which may be useful or may not.' How often when we do this, do we get home, see the list and say, 'Ah, now I remember what I really wanted... and I didn't get it'? We'd never walk into a supermarket and say to an assistant, 'Just give me anything.' We generally have an idea about what we want in advance.

Deciding what we want in the future, writing goals down, is a little like writing a shopping list for things we would like to have or happen in our future. Sometimes people think, 'Oh, but living life by chance is good; if we decide what we want, we might miss out on things.' Well, have you ever been to the shops with a big list and *not* also come home with a bag full of additional impulse buys that were not on your list? Writing goals simply means you get what you want and you get the surprises too.

If we don't decide and don't make choices, we leave life to complete chance not choice.

Choices

Kate, a wonderful lawyer I know, shared with me that it was only recently that she had started making decisions about what she really wanted. When Kate was at school, she was diagnosed with dyslexia and was told she wouldn't do well and wouldn't pass many exams. Kate decided to prove people wrong and went on to pass over 10 GCSEs with A grades. She had an illness at high school that further affected her performance and was told she wouldn't make it to university. To prove them all wrong she worked really hard and got a place at university. Kate was also told she wouldn't be able to study law because it would be too much. Again, she proved them wrong and qualified in law. What's interesting about Kate, now in her thirties and with a very successful career, is that when I met her, she was in a wonderful position where no one was telling her what she couldn't do any more, as everyone knew she would prove them wrong.

However, Kate felt that all the decisions she had taken in the past were based on proving someone else wrong, which is a pretty unique way of making decisions and generating the motivation to make things happen.

Now, with no one saying what Kate couldn't do, Kate had to discover how to create goals for herself, based on what she really wanted to do rather than on what others said she couldn't do. Kate needed to create a new shopping list.

Pot goals and garden goals

If you're unfamiliar with writing goals or it feels a little crazy right now to be thinking about how you would like life to be, or what you would like to do or have in five years, you can break your goals down into smaller time frames, for example the next couple of months. I call the short-term goals 'pot goals' and the longer-term goals 'garden goals'; the pot goals represent a season, things you'd like to achieve in the next two to three months, and the garden goals the goals of the future, which may take some time to mature.

Here is where this terminology came from and why we need both. Twenty-five years ago, several life-changing events happened in our family. My first nephew was born, I left home, my sister and little nephew moved to New Zealand and my Mum and Dad bought a field!

Dad would build a house on that field and Mum would create the garden. Mum had a vision for how this field, her new garden would look when she was finished. She started by spending hours each day just digging over a tiny piece of ground to prepare it for plants and grass. (In retrospect, she did say how much easier it would have been, had the field been turned over by a plough to start with; her back was never the same.) Armed with her trusty shovel, her first year was dedicated to preparing the ground for the following spring, when she would be able to start planting. Each year she did some planting, and the following year she planted more. It was about three years before her vision really came to life and all the plants, trees and shrubs became established. Three years after having her dream it had become reality and she could actually see what had once been only in her imagination.

It is a beautiful garden, and 25 years later it just gets better with every season. It brings me such joy to sit in her garden and I always think of her out there. She planted every shoot and cared for every plant. It was such hard work for her initially, but because Mum had a clear picture of what she wanted, every day was worth it, every piece of ground she turned over was worth it. This was always going to be her 'forever' garden and she was prepared to do all the hard work, even though initially she saw very little in the way of results (Dad is doing a great job of keeping it beautiful now).

As I mentioned, also 25 years ago my sister Vicki moved to New Zealand. We chatted recently about how tough it can be when you move to another country, especially one so far away and you have a newborn. Vicki told me how incredibly homesick she was in the first few years;

she said that every day she longed for home, missed us all so much and just couldn't see her future in New Zealand – thinking of being there long term made her feel anxious and nervous sick. The movie in her mind that was playing, not seeing us and being that far away from us long term, was unbearable.

So, she said she had to live her life in smaller chunks, and the way she helped me understand what that looked like for, her involved gardens. Not a surprise as Vicki had inherited Mum's gardening gene. Vicki explained that for the first couple of years, even though she had always loved gardening, she could not even contemplate doing any. Gardening for her had always meant planting things with the knowledge that the following year they would bloom beautifully. But the idea that she would be over in New Zealand to see the plants bloom the following year was actually too much, so she couldn't bear to plant anything. After a year or so Vicki allowed herself to do a tiny bit, but she said she only planted seasonal flowers in small pots as she could enjoy them in the moment or just for that season. She couldn't plant anything which might not flourish for a year or two as that was way too far ahead. Somehow, planting things which would come to life after that length of time might suggest she would still be there then, and she was only ready to live life in small chunks. So, she just planted pots and enjoyed them over that season.

It took Vicki five years before she began really considering planting anything which would flower the following year and, at that stage, she began planning a more established garden. Now, 20 years on, she has vegetable patches, chickens, horses, the lot; she finally managed to establish herself and her garden.

It is no coincidence that gardening is very much like life: we plant the seeds and wait for them to grow – just as we can plant the seeds of our goals and take steps to make them happen.

> To plant a garden is to believe in tomorrow.
> Audrey Hepburn

If you have challenges with creating long-term goals and visions of what you would like life to be like in the future, start by making very small short-term goals – pot goals that you can see the results of in two or three months. Vicki started off with seasonal plants before she progressed to the vision of the future garden.

When people are having a tough time, especially after a bereavement or major life event, such as a break-up, accident or redundancy, we tend to say 'one day at a time'. Goals in these situations become very short term, perhaps just to get you through that day still breathing. After a few days of achieving these immediate goals, we might imagine we can get through a week and then a month. Every goal you set, whether it's designed for the next five minutes or the next 50 years, can be celebrated when you achieve it – it's all progress. You can start with small pot goals and then, as your confidence grows in your ability to achieve what you set out to do, move on to longer-term life (garden) goals.

If you are not at the stage where you know exactly what you want, a great exercise to do is a life review; this is also good for making sure you're creating balanced goals which cover all areas of your life rather than just one or two.

Life review

There are many areas to your life – you have your work, your learning and personal development, relationships, family, holidays, finances, how you feel and your health. Undertaking a review of where you are now across all the areas of your life helps you consider what could enhance your life and enables you to understand what you want.

Exercise

Opposite, you will find a table which covers many of the different areas of your life. For each area of your life, imagine you have a scale between one and ten in terms of your levels of satisfaction. One is not at all satisfied and ten is 'wow, in this area of my life I am rocking'.

Think about each area of your life and give it a score out of ten. Once you have given a score, move on to the next column and consider the question: what could or would need to happen to make the score higher? It's this reflective element of the exercise that helps you figure out what might make you even happier in the future.

	Score out of 10	What would make it higher?
Career		
Love life		
Social life		
Family time		
Fitness		
Diet & health		
Wealth & finances		
Mind & well-being		
You time		
Fun		
Learning & personal development		
Holidays		
Possessions		
Home & surroundings		
Giving back & charity		
Helping others		

Once you have decided on what would make you happier in any given area, you will begin to gain more clarity on whether this is something you would like to create goals around in order to take control of your life and how you spend your time.

Your shopping list

Below is your opportunity to write down 20 things you would love to have, be or do in your life in the next year. Imagine it being a shopping list for life; in fact, it's your goals list and can contain how you want to feel, anything you would like to achieve or even own, new job, new house, feel happy…

You are 44% more likely to get, do and be these things if you write them down, so let's get writing. Use your wonderful imagination and for now don't worry for a moment about the how; don't let fear get in the way of writing down what you really want – we'll come to that in the following chapters.

Summary:

- Creating goals or your 'shopping list' is part of creating a future you're excited about.
- You can start with small 'pot goals' and move on to big 'garden goals'.
- We have lots of different areas in our lives; complete a life review to maintain a balance.
- If you don't write a shopping list right now, you might forget what it is you wanted.
- Deciding what you want gets you what you want and leaves room for surprises.
- New mantra: 'If you don't want, you don't get.'

Make it happen with your own movie. How many times have you seen a commercial for a beach holiday and thought, 'I want to go there', or seen the image on screen of someone driving a car and imagined yourself behind the wheel? If there is something you really want for the future, then this technique of *creating your own movie for the future is extremely powerful*. Become Walt Disney – dream big. It was Walt who said, 'If you can dream it you can do it!' And he is right; we just need to create the dream and your own image or movie to go with it.

Fearless goals

When I've worked with people for a while, we move on to the Walt Disney style of goals: dream big. I call the big goals 'fearless goals'; they are ones that when you achieve them will be life changing: deciding to retrain in a career, write a book, run a marathon, start a business, find love, climb Kilimanjaro. Have you noticed that whenever you see celebrities undertake a fearless goal, like climbing mountains for charity, they personally change as a result of achieving it? They have pushed themselves, had to train for it, met new people and done something they are proud of, and part of them has changed forever.

Jenny Hall, one of my clients and now a great friend, created just such a goal. When I asked Jenny if there was something she had always wanted to do, she was silent for a short while. Then, although Jenny says she doesn't actually even know where the following words came from, she answered: 'Sail around the world.' I had no idea Jenny was into sailing and I'd known her a long time. I asked her if she had ever sailed before, and she said, 'Never!'

When you create a fearless goal, the next step is to understand your why, your reason for doing it. Jenny said she wanted to be able to look back at her life and feel like it had been a success. I completed an exercise with Jenny where I asked her to fast forward and imagine herself at 90 years old, looking back at her life and her achievements. When Jenny closed her eyes and let her imagination picture her 90-year-old self, she had a vivid image of where she was. She described the image of a room in detail, and in this picture she saw herself surrounded by young children who were asking her about her life and looking at the photos she had on the walls around her.

In this mind movie, the photos on the wall represented her achievements and she saw a picture of herself on a boat on the high seas. The image was powerful and for Jenny was a perfect visual representation of her having led a successful life. It was this image which she returned to again and again while training for the round-the-world trip, which was extremely gruelling. When she was drenched and seasick the first time she went out on a boat, and when people questioned her about why she would take on such a huge challenge (one which others had lost their lives attempting), this was the image that kept her strong and helped her let go of fear. Jenny embarked on her 12-month trip around the world 18 months after she had created this powerful fearless goal.

You can create images as Jenny did of you in the future looking back at your life, imagine yourself at 90 what would you like to be proud of? Or for momentum you can also imagine yourself doing what you want to do. When you properly imagine yourself doing what you want to do or being where you want to be, you begin to feel the experience.

To create a movie you close your eyes and put yourself in the moment of achieving what you want. This is a common technique athletes use in their training; they continually imagine themselves on the podium being presented with a medal, or crossing the line first. Actors and actresses use this technique of future movies to imagine themselves making a speech after receiving an Oscar. To fully visualise it, they close their eyes and picture the audience in front of them; they feel the heat of the room on their bodies; they imagine hearing the applause and they listen to themselves making the speech. They fully imagine every part of the moment, activating all the senses, what they smell, hear, see and also how they feel; they imagine the feeling they will have when they receive that Oscar in the future.

The future movies you create fill you with love and excitement and the more often you play your movie over in your mind, the more real it becomes and the more you want it, the more you release fear and come from a place of love and are ready to make it happen. Your dreams and goals become part of you.

Here's a story of how this technique of using future movies helped turned Lisa's dream into reality. When I met Lisa, we were both attempting to get fit at an outdoor exercise class; we hit it off straightaway and were regularly told off for chatting in the class. Lisa had a great job – or at any rate a well-paid job – not a great one because it was highly stressful and involved working long hours. She would often be unable to make our exercise classes because of deadlines for proposals or other work, however much she needed exercise to help her wind down and relax. She fell into a cycle many of us will be able to identify with, of working flat out and having no time for life or for herself, followed by paying a fortune for a holiday to relax and unwind so that she could continue when she returned.

I hadn't seen Lisa for a few months and I was actually getting a little concerned as the last time I saw her, she had lost about half a stone in a couple of weeks, all through stress and hard work. When I did next see Lisa, she had just returned from one of these beloved and much needed holidays in Thailand and she looked fabulous, relaxed, bronzed and back to normal. As we ran around the field that night, she told me how amazing the holiday was and how she had talked with her husband about how fantastic it would be to go and live over there, to leave the UK behind and live in Thailand! They had discussed the idea of her husband becoming a diving instructor, as he loved diving. Moving to Thailand would be a very *fearless* goal, wouldn't it?

I asked her: 'Do you really want to move to Thailand?' The answer was yes, so the guidance I gave to Lisa was all about the images that she and Jon, her husband, could create to help make it happen. Clearly there are a lot of steps to making a move like this a reality, so this fearless goal would take time to realise. There would be plenty of time to face blocks, have fears, and maybe even suffer rejection. But one thing will always make this kind of dream possible, *your mind*, and if it's possible in your mind, it's possible in reality.

That night Lisa and Jon sat down and discussed what life would be like in Thailand, what they would do for work, what they would do in their spare time, and what they would feel like. Every part of the conversation at this stage was based on the *what* not the *how*. The how isn't important at this stage; if you jump straight to the how without a clear image of what you really want, you'll find this all-consuming, confusing, and it will create an immediate block in the process. Ultimately there is no way anyone who has never quit a job, sold a house, become a diving instructor or moved to another country will know how to do those things. Not knowing how to do something is one of the greatest fears which stops you taking action. We'll move on to all the how actions later in the book but, for now, it's all about the what.

Talking about the what of what life would be like in Thailand made Lisa and Jon really excited. They added into their discussions what it would feel like. They pictured themselves sitting on the beach, chatting, listening to the waves, clinking two glasses together and saying, 'We have made it.'

These kinds of future movies light up all your senses; every time you visualise the movie, you are in it, you want it. Trying out your future like this in your mind helps you decide: does this light me up? If it's a hell yes, you will make it happen.

Vision boards

Creating a vision board is part of changing your life and provides you with a future that feels good, that you want to move forward towards. A vision board is the place where you put all your goals and dreams in one place (everything you want to be, do or have from your shopping list). Once you have got some clarity on what you want on your goals list, the next step is to find images that represent those goals in order to complete and create your vision board. For Jenny who sailed around the world, she may have had an image of an older lady showing pictures to younger children, or of a previous yacht race leaving the harbour. For Lisa, it may have been a picture of a beach in Thailand.

Remember how creating images in your mind helps re-create your reality, to allow you to let go of fear and feel excited about the future. Having images on a vision board works in a similar way. Adding images to a vision board of your future 'wants' means that every day those images soak into the unconscious part of your mind and become a part of you. They keep your goals front of mind and put every part of you on high alert for opportunities to make them happen.

Creating your own vision board full of 'I wants' is very powerful. Trying to articulate exactly what you want can be a challenge, particularly if you haven't done it before, because you may not be aware of exactly what happiness and success look like. A vision board is where you place pictures of all the things you would like to have, be or do in your life in the future. This might be a destination you want to visit, things you want to own, a place you would like to work, the home you want to create or the people you would like to welcome into your life.

Any image can represent the things or feelings you would like to experience or own. I often use magazines or the internet to find the kind of inspirational images I like. The world is your oyster, and you can choose for your vision board whatever images mean something to you and represent the goals you have created. Once created, place your board in a part of your home where you'll see it every day. This will help you keep these powerful images constantly at the front of your mind, and you can regularly check in and visualise your goals becoming reality.

The images don't necessarily have to be of things you can personally achieve or even that you know how to achieve; you can add things to your board that represent everything you want for the future – material things such as cars, handbags and shoes, or experiences such as holidays, or any other things, such as love and laughter. What we want doesn't always need to be something we have to strive for.

When I asked Zoe what she really wanted, one of her 'I wants' was to see her sons getting along. They were 17 and 19 and she said they were constantly arguing and bickering, and it was getting her down. She took a photograph of them laughing and joking together and placed it on her vision board in the kitchen. Her boys passed the same image every day. They never asked why it was there, but within a week she noticed there had been a change in their relationship. The image of them laughing and joking together that they passed every day had soaked into their unconscious and their relationship changed; they were laughing and joking together again.

Another client placed details of a course she wanted to attend on her vision board. It was quite a pricey course but one she was very keen to attend. She didn't have the funds to pay for it at the time but remembered that a vision board is all about what you want in the future, not what you can actually afford now. Her vision board was in her kitchen. One day her cousin stopped by and was looking at the board while having a cup of tea. She asked about what the images represented; when she heard about the course and why her cousin wanted to attend it, she said: 'Let me pay for you to go on that.'

The year I decided to follow my core guiding principle of coming from a place of love not fear, one of the things I wanted was to fall in love again. I found two pictures that spoke to me. The first showed the feet of two lovers walking bare foot in the sand on the beach; this represented being in love to me. The second was a random picture of an actor. I was creating a vision board by flicking through magazines for images that would represent what I'd like in the future. I saw this lovely face looking out at me; he had stubble, kind eyes framed by thick glasses, a check jacket and a crisp white shirt. It just represented a picture of a man who looked nice (and turned out to be Jeremy Piven, the actor). A year later, when I met the love of my life, he had stubble, kind eyes framed by glasses and a check jacket and crisp white shirt. The similarity was uncanny, and I had to go back to the original vision board to double-check. When we were walking down a beach together that summer, I didn't think too much about it until I looked back at our footprints in the sand – that image from my board came back to me. You suddenly realise you are doing things you once dreamed about.

Vision boards are really fun to do with children. Consider asking them what things make them happy and adding pictures of those things. You can also use them in a work scenario and invite everyone to add an image of what success would mean to them in the next year. You could have separate vision boards for different areas of your life or a single board that includes everything. If you are decorating a house, you could put on images you like of interiors; this would be more like a mood board.

A vision board can be a place to add the goals you can work towards as well as crazy dreams that you would just love to come true. The key to a great vision board is imagination and not letting fear hold you back. Come from a place of love when you create one and imagine anything is possible.

Exercise
To create a vision board, make some time when you won't be interrupted; indulge in the process and allow a couple of hours. You will need scissors, a printer perhaps, magazines, glue, a large piece of paper or board and your goals.

Start daydreaming and think: 'If there is no limit to time or money, what would I really want and love to happen?' Capture your thoughts as images on your board. Once you have created it, you can add to it whenever you think of something new. Place it where you will see it every day to keep absorbing the images of what you really want. You will find it incredible watching these come true; the vision board really is the first part of letting the magic begin.

Summary of the I of the LIPSTICK principles – Imagine

- Consider what you would like to be proud of yourself for when you're 90 years old; what would you like to look back on as your best life achievements?

- If there is something you want in the future, create a movie of all that will happen when you achieve it. Imagine you can be there in the future moment – how does it feel? Then talk about it to everyone, imagine yourself there, and you're already taking the first step towards making it reality.

- Make a vision board with all the images of what you want to be, do or have in the next year or two; place it where you can see it every day and be ready for the magic to begin.

- New mantra: 'I'm ready for the magic to happen.'

PRESENCE

Presence from a place of love:

Being present from a place of love and savouring the moment could be compared to stopping for a moment, plugging your electric car into a charger, and filling up with energy for the next journey. Being present energises the mind and nourishes the soul. Being fully present with people creates meaningful, close, genuine connections which feel special. Being present from a place of love allows your mind to let go of worry, and feel clear. Creating space for new ideas and listening to your intuition. Being present from a place of love allows the answers to come and allows you to love life and feel you are in exactly the right place, just where you are supposed to be right now. It's a beautiful feeling of calm, confidence and belonging; you are connected with yourself, others and the universal energy around you. Being present stills the mind and removes doubt, worry and negativity.

Presence from a place of fear:

Presence from a place of fear is a head full of worry and stress; it's living in the past or worrying about the future. It's where self-criticism comes in and the eternal buzz of thinking and feeling you should be somewhere else or doing something other than what you are. It makes decisions difficult and our future fuzzy. It can create anxiety and stress, not just in our minds but also in our bodies and souls. Presence from a place of fear means we don't really connect with people as our mind is full of other things, doubt, lists and worry. This means we never really listen to, hear or see people or the world around us. It feels tiring and leads to sleepless nights and fatigue. Our minds are busy even when our bodies aren't, and we can start to make bad choices because our decisions come from a place of confusion and fear.

Our next LIPSTICK principle is P for Presence, and in this chapter you will learn how to be present in the moment, let go of the past and look forward to the future. You will learn different strategies for mindfulness and meditation and how to clear your mind. You will hear how listening to your intuition can lead to saying yes to experiences which could change your life, and you will learn how to be present with other people to create deep meaningful connections.

There is a real challenge for us these days, especially for the younger generation: the challenge of living in the moment. There are so many other places you can be without even moving. There is a new term that has emerged: *fear of missing out* (FOMO), which describes your state of mind when you are thinking about what else you could be doing or where else you would rather be than where you are. Social media and busy lives and schedules make it hard for us to feel really *present* or happy with where we are in the moment.

But it's not just fear of missing out; self-doubt and lack of confidence can also hinder us from being fully present. My mind used to be full of self-criticism and worry, which robbed me of the opportunity of feeling (and being) present. You can be a million miles away whilst sitting right next to someone. You can feel detached and distant even in a room full of people.

> Yesterday is history
> Tomorrow is a mystery
> Today is a gift
> That's why it's called the present

I had this poem printed on a t-shirt when I was in my twenties; it's always resonated with me and is more relevant now than ever.

Leave the past behind

The current average life expectancy in the UK is 84 years. In my seminars, I take out a big pink ribbon that I call *the ribbon of life*. I look around the room and ask what the average age is. It's often around 40, so I cut the ribbon in half. I discard one half of the ribbon on the floor and, in doing so, I make the point: 'That's the past, it's gone, and we will never get it back.'

If the past really is behind us, what are the good parts of the past you want to retain to take into the future? Certificates, qualifications, great memories. If we could package up all the amazing things from the past and take them with us into the future, that would be great, and we can.

It does us good to look back down memory lane sometimes and remind ourselves of fun times and achievements. There's nothing better than meeting up with old friends and having a 'do you remember when?' session. Reminding us of the laughs we have had and the antics, these sessions are great for the memory; life gets so busy that there seems to be very little time for reflection these days. I've got to say I do love Facebook for surprising me with memories from years gone by that would otherwise have been left in the past.

So that's the good times; yes, we love remembering these. But what about the times which weren't so good? The times that made us cry or sad or scared or hurt. What do we do when our mind likes to take us back to the past and memories we would rather forget? Taking these memories with us into the future is an obstacle for our success and happiness. When we struggle to let go of bad events from the past, we drag them around like a ball and chain, which drains us of our energy.

Today is today; we are all here living this moment and, as I said in my first blog post (see the Introduction), we are breathing right now. Right now everything is OK. Where we are in our minds can be very different; we can be constantly living in the past.

Utilising the future to help us feel good about what's ahead is vital for us to generate momentum and keep us moving forward. You will notice some friends may use the language of 'I can't wait' a lot, full of excitement about things in their diaries that they have planned; this is where future visualisation really works at its best to keep us happy. That's why we create goals and vision boards, so we can see bright events in the future we want to move towards.

But what if you live looking backwards and feel the weight of the past heavy on your shoulders, or find it hard to live right now in the moment?

Think of the past and the future as two diametrically opposed directions. Imagine for a moment that you are standing on a path: the future is ahead, and the past is behind you. You are facing backwards; you are looking back at the path of the past. You can't actually move backwards into the past, though, you have to move forwards. You feel stuck; you want to move forwards but you can't because you can't see it – you're facing backwards looking at the past.

You can't travel back in time so you have to move on, but there is a problem. The only way to move forwards would be to walk backwards; unless you can turn yourself completely around and look forwards, you would have to move in the direction of the future but without seeing it. You can only take tiny steps, and it feels awkward and uncomfortable moving backwards on the path. You cannot see the path of the future so you can't travel with energy; you can't run or skip towards your future because the path isn't in view to you. If you can't stop focusing on past events that you struggle to let go of, you will never move forwards towards your future because you simply can't see it.

To let go of the past you need to turn around and look forwards. So if you do find yourself looking backwards, it's time to turn around. Imagine yourself facing your past on the path and looking at it one last time and saying goodbye to it; wave goodbye if you like, and say goodbye out loud to be clear. Then physically turn around and face the future. As you turn around, imagine the ball and chain you have had anchoring you to face in the wrong direction being cut free, releasing you from events that have consumed too much of your present-moment thoughts. As you lose that heavy weight which has made you stuck, unable to move in any direction, you feel lighter as you turn and face the future. The path ahead into the future has nothing from the past on it; the sun is shining and the path is clear. At last you can feel the energy in your body return as you are now allowed to step forward, being able to see where you are going.

When we release the negatives from the past, we feel like different people.

When we've created some goals and images on our vision boards, we are able to see some of the great, bright, beautiful things ahead of us that we can now move towards because we can see them up there waiting for us.

Yesterday is history, let it go – turn around and face the direction that's bright and beautiful: your future.

Back to the seminar. The next thing I do is take the big pink ribbon of life and cut off a further third from the remaining length to represent the time we will spend sleeping. This leaves us with only a small length of ribbon.

It's now down to us to choose how we fill this small length of ribbon with things in life we want. Worrying about things that will never happen will mean your ribbon is shrinking and you're not living life to the full. Failing to let go of things that won't matter in a few weeks or months only serves to hold you stuck in that position, focusing on the past. Not letting go means shackling yourself to your ball and chain. Choosing which direction you want to look in comes back to our yes and no buzzers; we can choose to look forwards or choose to look backwards, and we can choose what we want to fill our ribbon of life with.

What else stops us feeling good right now in the present? Worry and anxiety will compromise the way we see the world so that the smallest things can seem so big and stop us enjoying the moment; being present is about the right now. When you are aware that a thought is creating worry, ask yourself this question: is this thought coming from a place of fear, or is it coming from a place of love? A fear-based thought causes tension, stress and unhealthy emotion; a love-based thought provides a feeling of calm and of being in control.

Sarah was arranging her wedding. She really wanted to enjoy planning the wedding and get really excited about it, but she was wasn't. She was building up to a high state of anxiety about the day and not enjoying the planning at all; she was frustrated with herself because she wanted to enjoy the whole process. Sarah talked through the thoughts that were running through her head which were creating the anxiety. She explained she was getting very worried about the day, and whether all the timings would work. What if she was tense on the day and couldn't enjoy it? What if others didn't enjoy it? The more Sarah thought, the more her anxiety continued to build; she was getting really, really worried that she would be anxious on the day and not enjoy her own wedding.

The question for Sarah was: was this thinking coming from a place of love or fear? She concluded that although her thinking had started from a place of love – it was her wedding day after all and she wanted the day to be perfect – her thoughts were now coming from a place of fear. Sarah wrote down all her worries from a place of fear and then again from a place of love.

Fear	Love
I'm really tense on the day and am not enjoying it.	I'm really relaxed on the day and love every moment.
I don't get the chance to chat to everyone and feel guilty afterwards.	I get quality time with everyone on the day and the next day feel full of love.
My guests don't enjoy it.	My guests love it and have a great time.
The timings don't go to plan and it cocks up.	It all runs perfectly and seamlessly.
My hair and make-up go wrong.	I love my hair and make-up; I'm so happy.

The next stage was to direct Sarah to put her fear-based worries in a box and leave them with me, and then take the love-based thoughts home to read every day. Sarah then created a movie in her mind of the whole day running perfectly to plan; she saw everyone smiling, laughing and saying what a fab day it was. She pictured the whole day and felt herself full of love. Sarah felt excited about her wedding again and remembered why she was planning the big day, a day about and full of love. Every morning when Sarah woke up, she read the love thoughts out loud, closed her eyes and pictured the day just as she wanted it to be. The more she did it, the more she knew this was the reality, and her anxiety disappeared and was replaced with excitement.

If you find yourself worrying or getting anxious about future events, write out all the thoughts that are coming from a place of fear, and then write a second list of those thoughts as if they came from a place of love, when everything will turn out perfectly. Now get rid of the worry thoughts; toss them in the bin or burn them ceremoniously, but they must go. This is a powerful action letting worry know you don't want it anywhere near you.

You come from a place of love not fear. Spend time reading out loud the love-based thoughts and create a movie of the future event going perfectly. Always have those love-based thoughts on you or around you and read them out loud. These are your affirmations and the more you say them out loud, the more the message gets through to your mind, and soon you have no worry thoughts at all.

Exercise

When you experience worry or anxiety, it is because your thoughts have become negative. When you notice this happening, ask this question: is this thought coming from a place of love or fear? When the thought is coming from fear, place your hand on your heart, close your eyes and use this mantra:

> I come from a place of love not fear, I come from a place of love not fear, I come from a place of love not fear.

This immediately brings you back to the present and calms you in the moment, regulates your breathing and stops any fear-based thinking. You are in control; you can stop those thoughts that cause you upset because you are in full control.

It takes time and practice, but the more you practise this technique, the more it will become second nature to you, and the great thing is that the more you say, 'I come from a place of love not fear,' the more quickly the fear-based thoughts stop visiting you.

Think of this new habit for letting go of worry as like refusing an invitation to spend time with worry.

Someone you're not that keen on calls and asks you out for lunch; you politely refuse, as you never feel good when you've spent time with them. They call again the next day and you refuse again. This continues and your answer is always no; it may take a little time and require you to be strong in your refusal, but eventually they stop calling and you feel at peace again. With this simple mantra 'I come from a place of love not fear' you are metaphorically saying to your thoughts, 'No, not today, stop calling,' and they will.

Live in the moment, and remember right now you are breathing, and all is well, and with your hand on your heart you can say, 'I come from a place of love not fear.'

Meditation

Meditation used to be associated with hippies and yogis in loose trousers and bare feet. Now it is something widely practised by everyone from prime ministers to footballers and athletes, and is taught to children in primary schools. Meditation and practising mindfulness are staple parts of your mental health tool kit.

There are hundreds of meditation apps to get you started. You can hop over to the website (www.thelipstickprinciples.co.uk) and download the 'revive in five' meditation, which gives you a first step into meditation and creating some *you* time. Other great apps to kick-start your meditation journey are Headspace and Calm.

I personally am a great fan of Deepak Chopra, who runs 21-day meditation programmes. You receive a new meditation into your inbox every day when you sign up to him. Sometimes starting on a 21-day programme is good because you can commit to 21 days more easily than thinking that this is for a lifetime; as you notice the benefits, you will want to do more. Be curious and find the apps and guides that work best for you. I have created a really easy 21 day meditation just five minutes a day, you can find the link on the website.

The reason audio meditation works is that the instruction from the audio gives your mind something to focus on other than your to-do list. In listening to an audio file, you are saying yes to five minutes of 'you time' and signalling to yourself that it's time to relax and have a calm moment. You want to feel present in the moment, right there and then, and having someone's voice to tune into really helps you do that.

Meditation doesn't work for everyone immediately. You may find it frustrating as you sit and wait for something to happen. Some people find it really hard and end up sitting thinking about anything and everything – the more they try to still their mind, the more active their mind becomes.

What you are basically looking to achieve with meditation is turning the busy thoughts in your mind off and just giving your brain a rest, for as little as ten minutes a day. The benefits of this are enormous:

- You learn to *see* your thoughts (the app Headspace is great for introducing you to this) because you notice your thoughts. You learn to have more control over them and recognise that they don't have to mean anything. This means that when you have a fear fantasy thought, you can control it more effectively. Once you get to noticing your thoughts, you can easily use the strategy of placing your hand on your heart and saying, 'I come from a place of love not fear,' to let fear thoughts go.
- You give your brain a rest. Just like any muscle, your brain needs some down time. Clearing your mind re-energises your soul.
- Clearing out the clutter from your mind means you create space for new ideas, new goals, new solutions. If your head is full to capacity with thoughts, there is no way fresh ideas can grow. If a room is filled with noise, there is no way of hearing a new tune.

I watched a documentary presented by Michael Mosley, a British TV journalist who specialises in biology and medicine. He was researching whether meditation can help to make you happy. In the documentary he said he was a self-confessed 'glass half empty' person, and he wanted to see if there was anything which could be done to change that. He had discovered during a previous documentary that his brain was actually wired that way. Of all the things he experimented with, it was the practice of ten minutes of mindfulness each day that actually rewired his brain so that he became a 'glass half full' and happier, more optimistic person.

If meditation doesn't work for you immediately, do not be disheartened. You can introduce being present into your world without actually having to listen along to audio meditation.

Mindfulness and being present

Being mindful is as powerful as meditation and, when practised well, creates the same effect of calming and clearing the mind. The beauty of mindfulness is that you can practise being present anywhere, without the need for sitting still and closing your eyes. You can refresh your mind and practise mindfulness in many ways, for example while walking (that's really good!), singing, dancing, doodling, drawing, doing sport. What you are looking to do is turn off your thoughts and tune in to the moment you are in. Walkers and runners often describe the activity as 'my mind clearer'.

I love festivals and skiing. I've noticed over the years that, on returning from both activities, I feel fully energised and refreshed. When skiing, there is only one thing on your mind: how to get down the mountain in one piece (especially for me as I'm not a great skier although I do love it). With this singular focus and the beautiful surroundings, it's easy to clear your mind of other worries or work.

Do you have a sport or activity that helps clear your mind?

At festivals, as you sit on a grassy hill in the sunshine and watch people, the colour and energy all around are mesmerising; this is a great form of mindfulness. People-watching anywhere is pretty cool; your mind relaxes as you float into a trance of observation.

Anything which takes you out of your everyday thoughts is a form of mindfulness. Even driving can be a form of mindfulness. You have the focus of the car in front and the road. Often on long journeys I find the mind clears of other things and so creates space for new ideas to pop in; some of my best ideas have appeared on long-distance car journeys.

It really can be anything that helps you focus in the moment and stops the background thoughts wizzing round in your head.

Walking in nature, surrounded by trees and greenery, is a great way to practise mindfulness. Try turning your focus to the countryside where you are walking. Really start to notice the detail of what is around you: the leaves on the trees, the birds tweeting or the silence. What you are aiming to achieve is a feeling of being present in that moment – it feels great and can lead to very profound states of being present.

A couple of years ago I experienced a very powerful moment of being present, really quite unexpectedly. It was 27 December 2016. I was at Mum and Dad's for Christmas. Mum was very poorly then with cancer and we had had a very beautiful quiet Christmas. I grew up in Bridlington, which is on the east coast of Yorkshire, right on the sea. That Christmas week had been crisp and sunny with bright blue skies, the kind of Christmas you wish for if you're not hoping for snow. On that day I woke early at around 5 a.m. As I lay there in the dark, my head was full of worry about Mum, and I was hoping the sun would come up soon, wanting the darkness to disappear. I thought of the sun rising and it occurred to me I had never actually seen the sun rise in Bridlington. Something in me, maybe intuition, told me to get up and go see it. So although cosy in bed, I got up, tiptoed around the silent dark house, made a flask of coffee and headed down to the beach.

When I reached the beach, I took a seat and looked out to sea in silence; I was really looking for a moment of calm. It was pitch black and freezing, there was no one around and the sound of the tide gently breaking on the sand was soothing. About a quarter of an hour later the black light began to change, and on the horizon a soft glow appeared out at sea, the glow appearing just ahead of the sun itself. Moments later the tip of the magnificent golden orange sun emerged and slowly rose up as if rising from the depths of the sea.

As I sat there, I was in awe of what I was witnessing and fully present in that moment. There wasn't a cloud in the sky to filter the sun, the tide was a long way out and the vast expanse of sand was rippled and wet; on the crest of every ripple, and in the pools of water in between, the reflection from the sun glimmered, giving the whole beach the effect of being a huge golden blanket. There was a golden blanket of light stretching from the sun to my feet, and somehow it felt to me as if this beam of light was able to connect me directly to the energy of the sun and to this incredible fresh new day dawning.

I was deeply touched by the experience, and incredibly grateful for life and the spectacle and beauty of nature. I experienced a profound feeling of well-being and peace, even though there were terribly sad things happening in my world; my mind was clear of everything except that moment. It gave me incredible strength to know there could still be glorious moments and peace even when there were other things to worry about. My overriding thought was that everything would be OK, and I felt immense peace and presence in that moment.

The other thought that filled my head concerned the amount of gold I could see all around me. The thought was this: here I am completely surrounded by gold and this makes me incredibly rich, incredibly rich. I knew this was a moment in my life I would never forget, and then a new mantra came to me as I realised that such moments, being surrounded by gold, feeling peace, are the riches we want in life. The new mantra that popped into my head is a constant reminder of where our focus should be: 'Make memories not millions.'

It was cold that day, it had been warm in bed, and on impulse I had decided to say, 'I'm in,' to an experience that I'd never witnessed before in my 45 years. It was beautiful and that image, that thought, that feeling is always with me.

I've seen that same golden shimmering in parks in the autumn when the leaves are on the ground and noticed the gold shining across the corn fields in summer. I have managed to experience that same feeling of complete presence many times and it's incredible. I am always able to connect with that state when I am surrounded by gold.

We are surrounded by so many riches; we just need to look up and appreciate them.

Being present and listening

You will have experienced the moment at a social gathering when the person you are talking to is looking over your shoulder and not fully making eye contact.

You know they are not really present with you, and it doesn't feel good.

I have been that person before, with one eye on the crowded room, half listening to people, because I'm wondering who else is going to walk through the door. I've also been the person chatting to someone and not really listening the whole time, because actually I've had a head full of other things, including on occasions self-doubt or concern about what I was actually going to say next.

Being present helps us connect with people in a more meaningful way; for me, it helps me feel genuine, calm and confident. The following strategies will help you to be present and help other people feel connected to you at the same time.

When it comes to being with people and having a conversation, there is the talking part of the conversation and the listening part of the conversation. Some say we are given two ears and one mouth so we can listen more and speak less. That said, there are many different ways of listening.

We have the over-enthusiastic listener who simply can't wait to join in the conversation, and when I say can't wait, I mean really can't wait! When one person is sharing a story or speaking, even before their last few words have been uttered, the over-enthusiastic listener has already started talking. Often their sentence will start with words of confirmation about how they have had a similar experience, or maybe with words of advice as they believe something they have just heard was in fact a cry for help. What you witness in the person sharing is that the tail end of their story melts away, as they have their message whipped from under them. It's not meant to feel that way for them; the over-enthusiastic listener just sometimes gets a bit carried away, and it can feel as if they weren't really listening so much as waiting for their opportunity to speak.

Then we have the under-enthusiastic or distracted listener who hardly makes eye contact or appears to be concentrating on something else. This is obvious to the person speaking, whether the conversation is face to face or on the phone. We've all done this at some stage. (Remember when we were younger and saw the person we had the hots for walk into the place we were in; we may have pretended to listen to the conversation of the people we were with, but really we were practising a different conversation in our heads in case he came over... Or maybe that was just me!)

Or perhaps you will recognise the disapproving listener – someone who is listening but whose facial expressions are signalling their disagreement or anger or their distrust of what you are saying. They are creating opinions on what is being said rather than just listening.

All these different styles of listening suggest that the person listening is struggling to be present for the other person in the conversation. Being present involves the ability to sit and listen without judgement, without waiting for our opportunity to speak, without feeling like you have to solve a problem and without having your mind on other things. Being present with people creates meaningful connections and, actually, when you are present it's a beautifully peaceful place, as your mind is only focused on the person you're with rather than on what you're going to say. You hear things in a different way.

To become present when listening, if you know you're a 'one eye on the door or on the clock person', sit with your back to the door or sit where you can't see the clock.

When you sit with someone, think about mirroring their posture. If they are sitting forward, leaning over the table, you sit forward leaning over the table. If they are leaning back, they may need some space so you should lean back too. When you display a similar posture to them, it creates an unconscious connection that we are the same.

Whenever you are in a social situation, put your phone away and turn off any distractions. Let those around you know they have your full attention and that you are physically present with them.

A few years ago, I met a guy called Danny, who invited me along to a session he was facilitating on deep connection and mindfulness. I said, 'I'm in,' and went along. There were about 20 people in the room, and he asked us to sit and face each other. Initially he had us focus on our breathing, which is one of the easiest ways to become present quickly. To do this, close your eyes, place your feet flat on the floor and breathe slowly – first, long deep breaths in through your nose, and then long slow breaths out through your mouth. If you repeat this five or six times, you may notice your body relaxing.

Now focus on your body and imagine doing a body scan as if there is a white light that starts at your toes and slowly comes up over your ankles, then your knees and on to the rest of your body. This focus on what's happening with your body in that moment makes you present in the moment. You can find this technique as part of our '10 minute mindfulness meditation' on the website www.thelipstickprinciples.co.uk.

Once we felt present with ourselves, Danny invited us to open our eyes and to look at and connect with the person opposite us. It was a very weird experience to begin with and not altogether comfortable. After a few minutes of my mind racing with thoughts about how weird it was, I settled into it. There was something about looking directly into someone's eyes that created an incredible connection; our breathing settled into a similar pattern and there was an indescribable feeling of calm and connection and safety in that moment. We all looked into each other's eyes for a very long time that evening, repeating the process again and again with different people.

I noticed that within a few moments of starting to eye gaze, my eyes would actually defocus and whoever was sitting in front of me would melt into a kind of fuzz, which made me feel very aware of my own presence. If your task is to look into someone's eyes to connect, it's pretty hard to get distracted by anything else in the room, and once you get over the strangeness of the activity, it feels amazing. I became a regular at this class and every time I left I felt fully energised, as we always will when we have managed to become present and clear our minds.

When connecting with other people, eye contact is king, though of course you are not going to sit and stare into everyone's eyes, and I don't think you need to in order to create connections with people. The key element of focusing on one person as the only person in the room will make you present in that moment.

Learning to be present in your life develops a peace of mind and well-being which will not only energise your mind, body and soul but also help you feel more connected to yourself and those around you.

Summary of the P of the LIPSTICK principles – Presence

- We can't stop time; life is passing by whether we like it or not, so let go of any shackles from the past and turn around and see the future.
- If fear thoughts of the future are consuming you in the present, put your hand on your heart, close your eyes, breathe and say: 'I come from a place of love not fear.'
- Say 'I'm in' to activities where you can practise mindfulness.
- Listen by allowing others the space to talk without feeling that you have to speak.
- Use your time with others to feel connected with them by being fully present in the moment.
- New mantra: 'Make memories not millions.'

STEP IN

Step in from a place of love:

When you have an idea or set a goal from a place of love, you are ready to explore the options, investigate possibilities, search out solutions and feel confident your action will result in progress. You feel you can back yourself and trust that everything will turn out just as it should. You can dare to dream big about goals that excite you so much you feel compelled to make them happen. You are committed to taking action and not afraid of making a mistake or going in the wrong direction. You are not afraid of failure as you know there is no such thing; there is only progress and you're ready to do whatever it takes to get where you want to be. Stepping in from a place of love means everything is possible and you are ready to jump off the cliff and learn to fly.

Step in from a place of fear:

Stepping in from a place of fear creates paralysis. Ideas appear but they're dead before they are even born, killed by the fear of failure or rejection, or both. Because the 'how to do it' isn't clear, the task of taking action feels too enormous so no action is taken at all. The challenge of *how* to make things happen is overwhelming and so dreams and goals lie dead in the water and never come to fruition, causing frustration and gradually eroding confidence that anything is possible.

Our next LIPSTICK principle is S for Step In. Here you will learn how to take action on your goals and move forward into making them a reality; you will learn that if you really want to do this, you will, no matter how nervous you are; you will learn the power of sharing your goals with others, and how important focusing on just one is.

As a coach and speaker I'm fortunate to meet and see women set bold brave goals, take action and achieve incredible things when they believe anything is possible. And they achieve this with two things: time and action. These are all you need to get where you want to be.

I host an event called 'Let Loose' where I chat with successful women about the key to their achievements. There is a common theme, which is that *they all take action* without worrying; they often describe it as jumping off a cliff without considering if they have a parachute. Having an attitude of coming from a place of love not fear means you can trust you will learn to fly once you've jumped.

I met Jennie Johnson MBE when she joined me on the panel of 'Let Loose', and her story blew me away.

Jennie was pregnant with her second child, worked in sales and wanted to find a great day nursery for her baby for when she returned to work. In her pursuit of this she discovered there was a huge gap in good quality, affordable childcare in her area; she visited loads of places but came out feeling all of them were not quite right.

This became a challenge for Jennie and was a potential obstacle to her returning to work and her future career. While considering this challenge on a train back from London, she had an inspired idea. If there was a shortage of great quality childcare, why not solve the problem, create the opportunity and build a new day nursery? Intuition or inspiration, the thought came from nowhere and during that two-hour train journey she gave it further consideration and came up with the name for a nursery: Kids Allowed. She jotted down as many ideas as she could on what might be involved in turning the thought into reality.

I have no idea what was on that piece of paper but it was enough for her to feel it was possible. The very next day she handed in her notice to the employer she was due to return to after the baby was born and began working out how to build a day nursery. Jennie literally jumped in and had faith that she would find out how to do it.

This style of action creates incredible momentum because as soon as you've jumped off the cliff, you will find out how to fly. Jennie took action – stepping in from a place of love means you take the first step without doubt, you have faith and you don't talk yourself out of it. You don't need to know everything. You don't need to know the exact route to where you want to get to. You just need to take the first step and not let fear talk you out of it.

Jennie has subsequently opened an additional eight childcare centres and has made a huge difference to thousands of people's lives – the children who attend, her employees and the parents able to return to work knowing their children are in safe hands. She even received an MBE from the Queen for her services to apprenticeships when she created an academy for apprentices starting a career in childcare.

Jennie's courage to step forward, and take the leap with that crazy idea that popped into her head on a train, changed everything. Jennie often says she feels that an entrepreneur's first course of action is to jump off the cliff and then figure out how the landing will take place. Her advice to all the women in the room that day was: don't spend time worrying about what could go wrong – you can only handle obstacles as and when they appear, you can't plan for them.

You never know where your action is going to lead. There is often no way you can fully plan the outcome as you only really see what's next when it gets to stage one. But what you can know is that when you're brave and you take the leap and act on your ideas and goals, you will learn, grow, change your world and likely the world of many other people. The world needs you to take action.

The focus of one

Last week someone shared with me that their goal was to lose six stone. Does six stone sound quite a lot? It's almost too much to think about. Half a stone is my goal – does that sound more doable?

In reality the two of us have the same goal to lose weight. When you break the task down into small, manageable bite-size chunks, we both have the same task, which is to lose a pound a week. If we both focus on this small achievable step and commit to losing one pound a week, we will both achieve our goals without feeling overwhelmed by the challenge. There is no way anyone can lose six stones in one week, but one pound is doable and manageable. The important part is getting started, taking one step.

When you have a big goal, never consider the whole, only the parts. It's all about just that very next step, that one thing you can do right now or today which creates the momentum and power to take the next step tomorrow. When you focus on the one pound, or the one action, it makes it so much more achievable. It's all the small actions that build up and take you to where you want to be.

Lily was starting out as a coach and said that, to have a meaningful business, she would need around 20 clients a month. As we chatted, Lily became quite overwhelmed by the huge task of finding 20 new clients for her business. When I asked Lily when she would like to have her business up and running, she replied, 'Ideally now'. From a standing start, getting to 20 clients is overwhelming and unrealistic unless Lily already had a list of people who have previously shown an interest in being coached.

Twenty new clients would also be overwhelming if they all came on board at once. So we changed Lily's focus to 'just one'. Where would her first client come from? Let's get one, celebrate that, look after them and then move on to the next one and so on. Everything starts with one – one conversation, one sale, one session at the gym, one pound.

Focus on the next *one* and continue until you reach your goal. There are two things between where you are now and where you want to be... time and action.

Remember Jenny from LIPSTICK principle 2 – Imagine? When Jenny decided she wanted to sail around the world, she had no idea how to do it or indeed if it was even possible for someone who had never sailed to find a way to do it. So the very first thing Jenny had to do was hit Google to find out how people get to sail around the world and who does it.

Once she had done that, making it happen was a series of single steps: finding a company that enables people to sail around the world; reading up on them; going to a meeting to hear about it; applying for it; getting accepted and then starting training; talking to her employer about taking a year out; telling her family about her mission; getting fit for the trip; buying all the equipment she needed; raising some money to pay for it. There were thousands of steps she needed to complete before Jenny could actually set sail.

With goals and action, you can only ever focus on the very next step in the process. You can't reach the end result without completing all the steps, and with every step you build a little more confidence and gather a little more knowledge so that you gradually get where you want to be. Just focusing on the next step, the goal for that day or that week, is enough to keep the momentum going and to prevent the experience from overwhelming you. An internet search is usually step one, whether you are starting a business, choosing a holiday, or even going on a date or finding courses. The minute you type into the search engine whatever it is you want to find out about, you have taken the first step. You can celebrate. There may be a million steps ahead, but you have completed the first one.

When you decide what it is you want or where you want to be, write your goal down on a piece of paper and write below that ten small activities you can complete to learn more about your goal or how to move towards it. These can be small steps or big actions. Ask your friends what they think; you'll find that ideas and momentum will soon come flooding in.

Put realistic timescales on your goals. If it is something you want to achieve quickly, take three or four actions every day if you can, but one a day will also get you where you want to be without overwhelming you. Remember always that anything is possible; your goals will become reality with two things... time and action.

If you want to, you will

Have you ever heard this quote from Henry Ford: 'Whether you think you can or think you can't, you're probably right.' It's always seen as a quote which helps people get in the right mindset for taking action. However, although I see some truth in it, I believe it misses the point. What I know to be true is that even when you *think* you can't, you often still do it (whatever it may be). Think about it for a moment; how many times have you said, 'I can't,' whilst actually in the process of doing something?

A few years ago it felt like everything was going against me in my business. Whatever I tried to push the business forward failed; nothing seemed to work. (On reflection I was probably trying to do too much in too little time.) One day, driving into town, a call came through to let me know that an event I was due to speak at had been cancelled; it felt like the straw that broke the camel's back. This thought popped into my head and it felt like the truth: 'I don't know if I can do this, I really don't know if I've got what it takes to do this.'

Then I remembered the Henry Ford quote – 'Whether you think you can or think you can't, you're probably right.' 'Well, Amanda,' I thought, 'if you think you can't do this, then you're probably right.' Then came a tight feeling in my stomach – self-doubt kicking in big style. Pulling over to the side of the road, close to tears, the fear of failure overwhelmed me. I felt crushed – if the thought was 'I can't', then maybe it was time to give up. Fantasy fear thoughts were racing through my head (when I used to do fantasy fear, I always did it very well).

Then, like a voice from above, I heard this question:

'Amanda, *do you want to do this?*'
'Yes, yes, of course I want to do this.'
'Well *if you want to, you will!*'

And in that moment I realised that whether you think you can or think you can't is irrelevant really, because if you *want* to, you will. There is only one question – DO YOU WANT TO DO THIS?

We will undoubtedly suffer setbacks when we head towards our goals. We won't get it right all the time; we may get it wrong more often than we get it right. But even if we take two steps forward and one back every time, we are still one step closer to where we want to be. I like to imagine this stepping forward and stepping back as the cha-cha-cha of life. We move forward, we step backwards, we step sideways sometimes; that's part of the dance, part of the fun. The important part is to keep on moving, keep on dancing the cha-cha-cha of life.

When you come from a place of love not fear, you won't have any of those crushing downward mental spirals, because you learn how to stop the disaster movie playing in your head, press pause, rewind and create the next movie, in which everything works out perfectly in the end.

Procrastination – what are you saying yes to?

Do you ever suffer with procrastination? Earlier in the book you were introduced to the ever constant yes and no buzzers; they come in very handy when dealing with procrastination. Think about those *things* that you need to do but you find it so much easier to do something else instead. Many a house has been tidied to avoid finishing a report for work, or a television programme watched to avoid tidying the house. The problem is that when you put off the thing you need to do, you'll find there is an unintended consequence. You'll start regretting your procrastination and berating yourself for it. This is a vicious circle that may start small but then moves on to more dramatic self-criticism.

Here is an example of this playing out. Helen said she felt frustrated at herself because she had been putting off doing some work on her business. She has a marketing company and loves loves loves loves working on her clients' marketing but never finds time for marketing her own business. Helen was asked what she was saying yes to and what she was saying no to by doing this. She said she was saying yes to getting client work done and having happy clients, but was saying no to growing her own business long term through ongoing marketing.

This is a constant problem for small business owners. You work hard on marketing, then you win a client and spend your time working for them. In doing so, you lose focus on further marketing of your business. When that contract ends, you are back to square one, starting marketing again. So having a constant process of marketing and lead generation is vital for future success.

The initial question was followed by asking Helen how putting off marketing her business was making her feel, and her answer was: 'I'm frustrated, I'm really annoyed with myself.' Helen wasn't just saying no to the work; she was actually saying no to feeling good about herself and yes to being frustrated and annoyed with herself.

When we can see that procrastination actually makes us frustrated, our reason for taking action changes. We take action because we want to feel good about ourselves; coming from a place of love not fear, we never want to be in a position where we can criticise ourselves.

Completing tasks will make you feel good. You know that feeling when you have spring-cleaned the house and you feel satisfied and happy. Completing tasks and taking action on what you have been putting off will spring-clean the mind and give you energy. Next time you put off doing something, remember you aren't just saying no to doing the task; you are also saying no to feeling good about yourself and coming from a place of love.

When working with people, one of the first tasks I'll ask them to do is a spring-clean at home. They make a list of all the little jobs in the house that need doing and put a date next to them for when they will be ticked off. (Obviously you don't have to do all the jobs yourself; you may have someone to help.)

When we get a little disconnected and out of sorts, it's likely we've let things slip; tidying up and spring-cleaning cleanses the mind as well as the house. As you tick off the list, you are giving your mind a very strong message: 'I get things done, I complete things.' The more you complete, the more you gain confidence that you get things sorted. Tidying a drawer that's needed a clear out will only take half an hour, but when you do it you are not only cleaning the drawer but also decluttering your mind.

Who knew that tidying and decluttering would actually raise your self-esteem and help you feel good about yourself! You're saying yes to a clearer mind, and the more space you can create in your mind, the more space you have for new ideas.

If you want to start creating goals and figuring out what you want in your life, do this one thing first: have a spring-clean at home so you feel refreshed and are starting with a clean house and mind. Be sure to throw out some things you don't use any more, especially clothes that haven't been worn for years; remember we don't want to hold onto the past. As you throw these things out, you are creating space for new things in your home and giving the message to yourself and the universe that you're ready for something new.

Now if you're still procrastinating, you will like this story. A lady puts in a weekly call to God: 'God, please let me win the lottery. Please let me win the lottery.' She then hears about vision boards and attracting what you want into your life, so she creates a vision board and places an image of a winning lottery ticket on the vision board. She asks God again, 'Please let me win the lottery.' Next, she imagines herself winning the lottery; she creates a mini-movie in her mind. She knows this is powerful and she runs that movie of her winning the lottery every day in her mind... Surely, that must do it? She asks God again, 'Please let me win the lottery.' Then she hears a voice responding to her; it's the voice of God: 'OK now lady, can you just help me out a little here and at least go and buy a ticket!'

Summary of the S of the LIPSTICK principles – Step In

- Sometimes you just need to jump and figure out how the parachute works once you are in the air flying.
- Break every goal into single steps of one and focus on the one.
- Remember – if you want to, you will.
- When procrastination kicks in, consider what you are really saying no to – feeling good about yourself.
- Do a spring-clean, cleanse your mind and create space for the new.
- New mantra: 'Between me and my goal are two things, time and action.'

TRUST

Trust from a place of love:

Trust from a place of love is having complete faith in yourself. You know you are on the right path and you trust that everything will turn out just as it should. Trust is a peaceful place, knowing you are living your life just as you should be. Trust from love is optimism and knowing that the universe has your back. It's having confidence in yourself to take a risk and know it will be OK. It's trusting yourself to say, 'Why not, what's the best that can happen?' It's saying yes, even though you're nervous, and trusting that whatever you're doing, it will have a positive impact on your life. It's grabbing life and saying, 'I'm in,' and yes, yes, yes to everything because you know there will come a time in your future when you won't be able to say that. It's listening to your gut and following your intuition and connecting with others and universal energy and acting on it. It's believing in something bigger than yourself that is conspiring to help you achieve what you want, and that little miracles happen around us every day.

Trust from a place of fear:

> Trust from a place of fear is doing the same thing every day and not trying new things or being open to the possibility of magic moments. Trust from a place of fear is believing the world is conspiring against you. It can leave you feeling exhausted, unhappy and disconnected, feeling life is all going to go wrong rather than all going to go right.

The LIPSTICK principle T is for Trust, and in this chapter you will learn how to tap into your intuition, and trust that the world around you, 'the universe', is supporting you, and how we can create 'good vibes' to feel happy and attract great energy back. You will learn about the law of attraction and creating lucky signs to give you faith that you are on track.

Have you ever had times in your life when everything goes your way? It feels like you are lucky and attracting great things – everything you touch turns to gold. Or have you had that tangible instinctive feeling that something good is about to happen and it does?

You could also have experienced the converse, a time in your life when everything you touched turned sour – one thing goes wrong after another and suddenly you're on a losing streak. We even have a saying when two bad things in a row happen; we say, 'Oh, bad things come in threes,' and for the next 24 hours we live in fear of what the next bad thing is going to be. We actually talk ourselves into bad luck and, hey presto, we get it.

When we believe bad things are about to happen, our energy changes and the vibration which we transmit out into the world changes – bad vibes. We are constantly transmitting energy from our bodies and receiving energy and vibrations back in. Quantum physics says that as you go deeper and deeper into the workings of an atom (basically all our bodies are just atoms), there is nothing there but energy waves – our bodies and cells are one great invisible force field which emits energy constantly. Each cell has 1.4 volts, which isn't much until you think of the 50 trillion cells in the body and get 700 trillion volts of electrical energy. This is what the Chinese call *chi,* and the energy can be measured outside the body to a certain radius.

Have you ever had an experience where you met someone and instantly connect but you have no idea why? Or perhaps the opposite – there was something about someone which instantly made you want to step away (bad vibes). This has a lot to do with the frequency of our vibrations; our vibrations may be completely in rhythm with someone else's, or the exact opposite, in which case our energy waves clash. When you are working flat out, with never a minute to stop, and your energy levels are at a high, it's pretty hard to connect with someone who is very laid back and chilled – you're on a different frequency.

The universe outside of us is also energy – everything from the plants and the trees to the houses we live in, all vibrating away and creating an energy and atmosphere which we will either like or not like.

Have you ever walked into a room where two people have just had a row? They are both smiling, so not giving anything away, but you can feel the tension, even when you can't see it.

Given that everything is energy, including us, we can start to think about what energy we are transmitting and also what energy we are attracting. A client who was having a tough time, with lots of challenges and obstacles being thrown at her, said, 'I don't know what energy I'm putting out there at the moment but I am attracting all the wrong things.' This level of awareness is fantastic, but how do you change it? How do you reverse it and start emitting good energy and attracting great things to yourself?

Remember back in LIPSTICK principle 2 – Imagine – how you learnt about how our thoughts create images, which in turn lead to feelings and emotions? We use the same method to create good energy. We focus on what's good in our world, the things we love, and fill our minds with future positive images from our vision boards and with mind movies of events in the future we are excited about.

You learnt in LIPSTICK principle 3 – Presence – about mindfulness and meditation; this is all part of your tool kit for maintaining your positive vibe. The daily habit of placing your hand on your heart and repeating your mantra of 'I come from a place of love not fear' will help maintain your good vibes. Being out in nature among trees and greenery, which is all emitting its positive energy, helps fill you with positive energy. Remember the story I shared about the sunrise, and how the path of golden sunlight from the sun to myself filled me with positivity and energy. You may be different from me in terms of what fills you with positive energy and how you like to spend your time, but the staples of your mantras and meditation plus spending time doing things you love, will keep you on track.

Surround yourself with positive people who transmit at the same vibration (vibes) as you (you know who they are) and don't spend time with anyone who doesn't. It's about more than just not enjoying their company; those people on a different vibe from you can affect your frequency, as the two energy waves clash.

At a very basic level, if you feel your vibes are feeling more bad than good, then a simple fix is moving your body, giving your body a really good shake about. My preferred method for this is putting on a song I love and singing along and dancing to it. Three minutes rocking a great tune and 'dancing like no one is watching' creates a different vibe immediately.

As you become more and more aware of your vibrations, you will begin to notice what you are transmitting and what you are attracting. You will begin to feel energy, your own and other people's.

Law of attraction

The law of attraction is described in detail in the movie and book *The Secret*, written by Rhonda Byrne. If you haven't read this book or watched the movie, give it a go. The law of attraction involves three steps:

- ask
- believe
- receive

Ask for what you want, believe you will receive it, and then celebrate the heck out of it when it happens. It works on the premise that if you take time creating energy and focus around something you really want, you will attract that into your life.

It's simple: get really clear on what you would like to happen in your life and what or who you would like in it, and create the images and movies in your mind which represent what you want. In doing this, you are:

a. getting super clear on what you want
b. giving yourself a constant reminder of what you are looking for

We have looked at this in more detail in LIPSTICK principle 2 – Imagine – using vision boards.

Our minds are in effect a goal-seeking device, looking to help us achieve what we really want. It makes sense therefore that if we focus on future goals and what we want to achieve, our minds will be on high alert for opportunities to help us achieve this.

Deepak Chopra, author and prominent figure in alternative medicine created the term 'synchro destiny' – harnessing the infinite power of coincidence to create miracles. This is the connection between knowing what you want and being aware enough to see the opportunities around you to achieve it; often these opportunities can seem almost like small miracles or incredible coincidences.

The key to all of this is the ability to future focus and make decisions about what you want; there will never be an incredible coincidence or little miracle if we haven't been able to ask for what we want in the first place. What you want doesn't have to be a new house or handbag or job. You might want a family member to call, or to meet someone who knows how to build a website, or a new customer.

Once you know what you want, you are able to ask for what you want, to verbalise it, and then the magic begins. You can start to use your energy and good vibrations to attract it (just like in the past when you have been on a lucky streak).

I'd call this asking the universe; my sister would say you're asking God. My sister Vicki is a Christian and so when she decides to talk about her goals, she tells or asks God.

For me, it's not so important where or to whom you direct your request. The important part is being clear on what you are asking for, being super clear on what you want. Once you are able to verbalise this with clarity, you can ask the universe, God or a friend, or you can stick it on Facebook or social media; the power of asking for what you want, and believing it will appear, are what's important. In the next LIPSTICK principle – Inviting Others In – you will learn how the more people you speak to and ask for advice, the more your percentage of success goes up. In this principle we are focusing on the element of putting your trust in you and the universal energy around you.

When I talk here about being clear, it looks like this. Would you like more money? Most of us would raise our hand for this. So, let's say we ask the universe for more money, please, and we put the energy out there and believe we are going to get it. Next day we are walking down the street and there is a one-pound coin on the path; we pick it up. Do we celebrate and thank the universe or do we review our order and say,

'Thanks universe, but actually what I meant was I'd like £1000 to come my way'?

Clarity is key.

I sometimes have fun with clients around engaging with the universe. They have to think of something that would be great to happen, which would surprise them out of the blue, something that would be cool, and I have them ask out loud for it, putting in a request to the universe. They then imagine that whatever they are saying is going to be carried off on the wind. When the wind finds the person their message needs to go to, the request will be heard. We even go outside into the open air and play at throwing the request out into the air, letting it float off to wherever it needs to go.

We are all busy in our lives and haven't got time to focus on everything, so leaving some space for a little bit of magic to happen that the universe can take care of is an easy option. Requests that have gone out and been carried on the wind include: 'my daughter will call; she hasn't called in a long time', 'the love of my life will appear', 'a new job opportunity'. One of the best was when a client of mine said she'd quite like to make a travel programme for TV (she worked in the travel industry but not on TV); three months later her business was contacted by a TV producer, and she was asked if her travel company would like to be featured in a new documentary.

There is nothing more magical for me than when a client has sent these requests out on the wind and then later I pick up the phone and hear the words: 'Amanda… you are not going to believe this…' And they go on to explain that the magic has happened.

We leave room in our world for a little bit of magic, and this is where trust comes in; give it up to the universe and trust that it will happen.

1. Get clear on what you want (even some crazy things).
2. Say it out loud – throw it to the wind if you like, as if you're sending the request off.
3. Leave it to the universe.
4. Be ready when it comes.

Remember that the universe and our energy transmitters work in all kinds of different ways, like when you're just thinking about someone and they call; you're just chatting about a friend and then you bump into them on the street; you just mention to someone you're thinking of joining a club and the next person you meet tells you about a club they have just joined.

Note: To play your part in keeping the universal energy moving, we have to respond to energy coming our way; remember you might be receiving requests from other people who have put things out to the universe. To play your part, when you think of a friend you haven't heard from in a while, call them. If you feel a sudden urge to go somewhere and do something, do it. If you get a strong sense that something is right, it is. Follow your intuition, it's the universe calling.

Sliding doors

A great friend of mine has been single for a few years and was quite happy with that, but this year she decided she'd like to meet someone. She entered the world of internet dating and the first couple of weeks were not positive. Some of the messages sent to her by unsavoury blokes were not for the faint hearted. But she persisted in the hope that a 'normal' guy might turn up at some stage. She got chatting to one man who seemed nice and normal. He was working in the area and said he would stay on for Friday evening if she would like to go for dinner. Nervous, as this was her first date in a couple of years, she said, 'I'm in,' having decided she would be open to saying yes to more things.

They arranged to meet in the bar of the hotel where he was staying. When she arrived at the bar, she texted 'I'm here' and ordered a Prosecco. To her surprise she received a text back saying 'Come up to my room'. Obviously she said, 'I'm not coming to your room, I'm in the bar.' The guy was persistent. My friend couldn't believe it. This normal-seeming guy was thinking she would go into a room with a stranger. She texted him to say she was leaving and finished the Prosecco. Gutted, shocked and surprised, she headed for the hotel foyer to call a cab, thinking all the time, 'Honestly, my friends won't believe this.'

In the hotel foyer the revolving doors swung round and out stepped a very handsome guy she recognised. Fifteen years ago they had had a conversation at the gym and she had always remembered him. She took a chance and said, 'Hello.' He looked surprised, so then she said, 'We chatted a couple of times at the gym.' When he asked what she was doing there, she said, 'I'm just leaving, I've been stood up.' The chap looked concerned and asked if she was OK, and then said, 'Would you like a drink?' At this point she thought about saying yes to things, trusting the universe and her new mantra 'I'm in', and she said, 'Yes.' They ended up having dinner and have met again since.

You never know what is around the corner (or in the revolving doors) – have faith, trust yourself and trust the energy; everything will work out well.

There are signs everywhere

When Mum died, I travelled home most weekends to see Dad; we both needed each other. As it's a six-hour round trip, I would listen to audio books. I've always been a fan of audio books and decided not to go for my usual choice, what you would call 'work audios' designed to teach me something. This time I'd try fiction instead. As I tuned into Audible, a title popped up: *The Universe Has Your Back* written and recorded by Gabrielle Bernstein. 'That's funny,' I thought, as just that week work had been going really well and I'd said to a friend that I was feeling as if the universe was supporting me through this tough time. It was as though the universe had my back and was guiding me along. I decided this was a sign, 'a happy coincidence', and, following my intuition, downloaded the audio book and set out on my journey home.

Gabby Bernstein is a Spirit Junkie (the title of another of her books) and has great faith in the universe. In the audio book she was talking about interacting with the universe – asking for signs to help guide her when she needed help. This was interesting to me as, following Mum's death, I'd developed a real belief that the sight of white feathers would mean Mum was close by, and I took real comfort in that. So when Gabby was speaking about having a sign or a spirit guide in your life, such as an animal, it was easy to make the connection that a sign could work like a white feather. My partner does the same with little robin red breasts, and we use the phrase 'when robins appear, loved ones are near'. His robin is the same as my white feathers; we both feel loved ones are near when we see them.

It's comforting to see these signs, and often they appear just at the perfect moment.

What's your sign?

Gabby was coming through the car speakers and encouraging me to interact with the universe. She suggested that if you identify a symbol or sign which has meaning for you, then when you feel the need to ask for reassurance, the universe has the opportunity to show you that sign. At first, I couldn't decide what my symbol was, and then an image of Mum came to me. In it she was smiling and wearing a lovely jumper with a flamingo on it. 'OK,' I said, 'my sign is a flamingo; go ahead and show me a flamingo.'

I travelled about another quarter of a mile and turned a bend. On the bend was a building, on the side of which was an old advertising poster for a nightclub with not one but two flamingos. This was my turn to think, 'Amanda... you won't believe this.' My sign was most definitely a flamingo!

Once you've decided on a sign, what does it do? When you see your sign, it feels as if you have a marker telling you that you're in the right place, this is where you should be right now – some kind of mental and spiritual guide, something you can trust to reassure you that you're taking the right step.

The following weekend, after my flamingo moment, Dad and I were doing a tour of junk shops and antique places. I'd seen a dressing table on Pinterest. The price was extortionate so I'd decided I could probably re-create it with an old dresser. We went to three different places and looked at lots of furniture, but nothing was turning up. The next place we walked into looked more like a huge jumble sale. 'We definitely won't find it here Dad,' I said, feeling a little shopped out, and decided we shouldn't even bother with this place. 'I'll just nip to the loo before we go.' On the back of the loo door was an old newspaper cutting and in the picture was a flamingo. 'Dad,' I said, 'I think our dresser might just be here.' With this sign and faith and renewed energy we started looking. We didn't find one dresser, we found two. Without the guiding sign we would have left and I would probably have given up on my dresser forever.

After that, I started seeing flamingos everywhere.

Helen, who attended one of my events, decided her sign was a black and white cat. She had just started house hunting and the next day was viewing three. In the front garden of the second house sat a black and white cat. There was just something about that house. She ended up buying the house and, as an added bonus, started dating the guy who sold it to her. There should have been two black and white cats that day!

Decide on your sign and then request it when you need it, or look for it when you need reassurance and confidence you're on the right track.

Signs can be even more obvious than this. Once, driving down the motorway in the pouring rain, I'd been thinking about taking my business online. To be honest, I'd thought about it a lot and every time I thought about it, I got frustrated. It felt as if I would be running a technology business rather than a coaching business. Struggling with this decision, I decided to work with the universe for the answer: 'OK, universe, if it's the right thing to take my business online, if that is the *right* decision, give me a sign.' If the universe didn't give me a sign, I figured I was off the hook. I couldn't see how a flamingo would appear anytime soon on a motorway in the pouring rain in the middle of Manchester. Immediately afterwards, within about 90 seconds, a car pulled in front of me from the next lane and through the rain I saw its number plate: W RIGHT 1. And so I made the decision to take my business online!

At an event recently an audience member asked one of my panel, 'What do you do when you don't know what to do?' Jennifer Atkinson, the panel member, who is an extremely successful entrepreneur, said: 'We all have the answers… the answers lie within. We just need to listen to our instinct, get quiet and trust what you know.' When you get quiet and clear your mind of clutter, when you act in the present, the answers will always come. If you ask for the answer, the answer will appear; trust it will.

Imagine the universe like one big Amazon website. You type in the request and it will arrive. (Obviously you don't get a specific delivery date; you have to keep your eye out for its arrival.)

Time and again I see people order from the universe and then fail to recognise the order when it arrives or, even worse, change their mind when it finally comes.

A friend recently decided she wanted to start dating again. With encouragement, she put it out on the wind for the universe to take care of. A couple of days later, a work colleague mentioned they had a friend who was looking to start dating again – would she be keen? Guess what my friend said: 'Oh, no! I don't think so!' Suddenly fear got in the way and she cancelled her order. You can't order a pizza delivery and then, when the pizza shows up, say you are not hungry! You ordered the pizza… never turn the pizza away.

Everything you are learning in this book is about helping you let go of worry and fear, live in the moment and love life. With every strategy you implement, you trust more and more, release negativity and feel massively positive about the future. You learn to trust that everything will turn out OK, in fact better than OK because it will turn out more or less as you planned it, and you can live life from a place of love not fear.

Summary of the T of the LIPSTICK principles – Trust

- Follow your intuition; when something pops into your life and it seems a happy coincidence, notice it.
- Work with the universe and decide on a lucky sign.
- Get super clear on what you want, throw it out on the wind and trust the universe will deliver.
- Never cancel the order; if you ordered pizza, accept the pizza – it will come.
- Always say, 'I'm in,' as you never know what might happen when you say yes.
- New mantra: 'I trust the universe is working with me.'

INVITE OTHERS IN

Inviting others in from a place of love:

This is a warm and wonderful place where you
realise you don't need to have all the answers
because you are surrounded by supportive, positive
people who want to help you and will share their
ideas and advice when invited. Inviting others
in involves: feeling confident to ask for help and
knowing that vulnerability is sometimes the greatest
strength you can show; being open to alternative
solutions and not feeling as if you have the world
on your shoulders; being comfortable meeting new
people and discovering where the people who can
help you hang out, and being excited to welcome
new people and perspectives into your world. It's
finding your tribe.

Inviting others in from a place of fear:

This is a lonely place where fear of judgement takes
over and you are unable to ask for help. A heightened
sense of responsibility leaves you feeling stressed
because sometimes you don't have the solutions
but feel you should be providing them. Not giving
other people the opportunity to help and support

you leads to them feeling rejected or that you have a barrier around you. People may think it's your way or the highway and give up offering to help and support. It is a feeling that you are alone on this journey of life and you have to do everything for everyone or nothing will get done.

This I of the LIPSTICK principles is for Inviting Others In, and in this chapter you will learn that inviting others in, not being afraid of rejection and finding your tribe are vital to your success and happiness. You will learn that you don't have all the answers and you don't need them; all you need is to be brave and invite others in to help you to get where you want to go.

There is something we all need to remember to have a happy, connected and successful life. We need people. We need help and support; whatever you are trying to achieve, someone somewhere will have the answers you need.

When someone invites me to work with them, it's because they know they would benefit from some help and support to achieve clarity and take action to get where they want to be. It's no coincidence that coaching is often requested by the women at the top who are already experiencing high levels of success that they wish to maintain.

We don't need to be at the top or have a coach to achieve success, but we do need people. Whether you are a new mum or starting a new business, a fresh sporting adventure, a new way of thinking or something new like mindfulness, whether you are experiencing grief, writing a book, or whatever it is, it will be easier and more effortless with the right people around you.

Over the years I have noticed that asking for help, admitting we don't have the answers, is a difficult hurdle for many to cross. For some crazy reason, people won't ask for help or they actually even turn down help when they need it most. Yet those that do ask are the ones who get where they want to be faster and with greater ease.

The dream is a dream team.

When starting my first coaching business, the hardest thing was the sense of being alone. Used to working in a big organisation with a huge team, I found it tough. I'm a sociable person, much more extrovert than introvert, and yet I'd decided to go it alone in business to fulfil my purpose of helping others feel great. There was no clear picture at the time of where the business was heading, just a huge amount of passion to make it work. I was used to working with other people and bouncing ideas around and I loved that, coming up with solutions and plans together.

Now I was creating the strategies and I was everything else too: the accounts department, the sales department, the marketing department and, let's not forget, the coach! Looking back (and hindsight is a great thing), it's clear I could have made things much easier by inviting others in to help. It was tough some days at the start, really tough to know which was the right direction. I didn't know about these principles then. I wasn't applying LIPSTICK. These success strategies came later. Just because I was a good coach didn't mean I was great at marketing, accounts and sales. I made a lot of mistakes, spent time on things that were not important and exhausted myself trying to do it all.

I always had one person with me and for that I'm eternally grateful. That was my Mum. Mum lived a few hours' drive from me so our contact was more often on the phone than in person. When the chips were down and I couldn't see the wood for the trees, I'd call the hotline (which we lovingly named 'the bat phone') to Mum. She was always supportive and ready to listen to me talk through my challenges, and I felt her love during every call. However, although Mum could love me, she wasn't in business and hadn't a clue what I was talking about most of the time. She'd say, 'I just don't know how you do it,' and on occasion, hearing my frustration and exhaustion in the face of lack of progress, she'd ask: 'Would it not be easier to go back into the corporate world and get a salaried job?' Mum just wanted me to feel good and not have to push through all the personal boundaries and hurdles you face when starting a solo business. I'm very grateful for having the number for the 'bat phone' and the support I always received, but it could have been very different. I could have had support from people who were really able to help me in the business.

Why didn't I ask them? For a mixture of reasons: firstly, I was not as aware then of the power of asking for help and, secondly, fear – fear that I would look stupid or as if I didn't know what I was doing (even though I didn't!) – plus a bit of 'well, I've decided to do this, I must have all the answers'. Wrong, wrong, wrong.

It's actually frustrating to look back and realise how my progress and success were inhibited by not opening myself up and inviting people in.

Find your tribe

Finding our tribe at the time we need them most is powerful. We have to find the people who can help us – who is your network, who is your tribe? There are hundreds of clubs, memberships and networks to tap into, and there are joint working spaces so if you work alone you can connect with others in the same situation. Someone somewhere has done what you want to do; they have the answers or they have an opinion that may be able to help you when you get stuck.

I run 'masterminds' in my business where groups of women come together and share advice and ideas on how to get moving faster. It's incredible to hear the variety of solutions to challenges or ideas for action that women from diverse backgrounds and careers come up with.

So why don't we reach out and ask for help? Maybe we don't know who to ask or perhaps we feel vulnerable, or maybe we just reject ourselves first. Coming from a place of fear would have us believe that people won't help, or we may imagine they would think we are stupid so we say no to asking rather than coming from a place of love that there will be the help we need.

I love this little poem; it's a very powerful statement when considering your tribe.

Some people come into your life for a reason
Some people for a season
And some for a lifetime

Throughout your life you have met loads of people who have helped and supported you in different ways. At school there were the teachers and adults who showed you the way, kept you safe and gave you advice on life. After leaving school, you meet a new set of people through education, travel and work. You have colleagues who support you, maybe managers who encourage you, and friends who are into the exact same thing as you, who you love spending time with and make you feel good. These people and support networks change, just like the seasons. But everyone, everyone has been in your life for a reason. There are probably a ton of people who have helped you on your path and you may have even forgotten. Sadly we just don't retain every moment in our lives.

As we grow, we need different things. Do you remember as a young adult when you thought you knew it all? Then later you returned to the incredible advice adults had.

There are people who come into our life and stay with us a lifetime. Others you know for a very short time at a specific point in your life when they come into your life for a reason.

Through all my studies I've met incredible people. Remember Rob from my NLP? Over the months we studied together and fulfilling careers, we were there for each other; no one else I knew was going through the same thing. Then in time such a relationship can drift because the reason or the season has passed for your friendship.

A goal shared is a goal that becomes reality

You know the saying 'a problem shared is a problem halved'; it's true. I have another: *'a goal shared is a goal that becomes reality'*. A super quick way to start making your goals a reality is to take your first steps towards sharing your goals with other people and inviting them in to help. Once you have shared a goal with someone, the next step is to go out and tell anyone and everyone what it is you want to achieve. My theory is that the more people you tell, the more likely it is to happen. I haven't yet had this theory disproved. Sharing your goal with:

one person = 10% more likely to happen
two people = 20% more likely to happen
three people = 30% more likely to happen
four people = 40% more likely to happen
five people = 50% more likely to happen
six people = 60% more likely to happen
seven people = 70% more likely to happen
eight people = 80% more likely to happen
nine people = 90% more likely to happen
TEN PEOPLE = YOUR GOAL WILL HAPPEN or your solution will be found

Here's how it works. Firstly, if you have shared your goal with one person, it may well be the first time you've said it out loud. It can feel weird saying what your intention is out loud. You may feel nervous about sharing with someone, worried about their reaction. This is often the stage where you may use language such as 'I'm thinking about starting my own business' or 'I'd love to study' or 'I'm thinking about going travelling' or 'I'd like to have a go at stand-up comedy'. You are likely to test the water by stating your intention as a wish or a possibility. At this stage, you are not totally committed. It's more of a 'maybe one day'. Depending on the reaction you receive, you may gain confidence and be encouraged to talk about it more.

When you next share your goal, you are likely to be more confident so that you now say, 'I'm wanting to start my own business.' This will feel different to you; it's now more definite – not completely certain but you are starting to anticipate the outcome. When you say it out loud, it's still a little scary but it feels a little more real. People begin asking how you are going to do it and showing interest in what you are doing, even offering tips and advice.

This is where the magic starts.

The next time you say it out loud, you are likely to have added more detail to the intention or the goal. 'I'm going to start my own business *next year*.' At this stage you are forming a picture of doing it, sounding confident and, more importantly, feeling more confident that your plan may actually happen. With the third person you talk to, you are sounding so much more definite that they are likely to believe you are going to do it and offer words of encouragement: 'Good for you, I'd love to do that.' At this stage the momentum really starts to build in you. The person you are talking to may ask questions about how, where, what, and in response to every question they ask, although you may not know the answer, you either miraculously come up with an answer or will be encouraged to think: 'Actually I had not thought of that, I'll find out.' Other people's questions around what you are going to do will help you formulate your ideas and plan how you are going to do it. You don't need to have the whole plan in place before you start to share parts of it; the process of sharing helps create the plan.

This is also the stage when those around you begin mentioning other people they know who have done something similar and sharing their stories with you. At this stage, you've shared your ideas with three people. In all likelihood it's probably only the third person who really believes in what you are planning, as you will have grown in confidence with each telling (hence the 30% more likely to happen at this stage). Everyone knows someone who has done something; you are finding the person who knows someone or knows something, or who asks the right questions or gives the perfect encouragement.

When you arrive at the fourth person, you may well have an even better formulated plan and by now you are beginning to select the people with whom to share your developing goals: 'I'm going to start a business selling cupcakes. It's going to be an online business and I'll cater for children's parties and events such as weddings and christenings.' If you get really clever at this stage, you will follow this up with: 'Do you know anyone who has set up a business who may be able to give me some advice?' Or if you are feeling particularly brave: 'I have no idea exactly how to make this all happen, at this stage; do you have any suggestions?' The more you talk about your intentions and goals, the clearer the picture becomes, the more gaps get filled in.

By person number five, you are really feeling it and starting to understand what you need to make the dream happen. The more specific you become in terms of what you are going to do and the support you might need to make it happen, the more your friends, family, acquaintances and the universe have the opportunity to help you with it. Coincidences, little miracles, start to happen and the path to your destination begins to open up in front of you.

At this stage, you are able to say: 'Next year, I'm starting a business. I'll be selling cupcakes for weddings and birthdays and also selling online. I am planning bespoke cupcakes carrying personal messages, all delivered in person, rather like a bunch of flowers. I want my business to put a smile on people's faces. I will deliver to workplaces. I'm going to need help with a website and want it to be really creative and beautiful. I'm also going to need a small shop in an appealing area, where people can come and sample the cupcakes and where we can bake them. I need all the help and advice I can get right now. Do you have any suggestions?'

Once you get specific about the areas where you want help, you should find people who can actually start to help. What is happening is that you have activated something in their brain called a reticular activating system (RAS), which is a solution-finding device. The greater the number of RAS's you activate (i.e. the more people with whom you share specifically what you want), the more solutions will come to you. People love to help and support other people; it's a natural response in all of us.

Imagine chatting to a friend over coffee and mentioning you are going shopping later to look for a new dress, quite a common chat among friends. Your friend mentions she wants some new shoes and may see you later at the shops. You both go off to the shops and walk past all the shop windows full of dresses and shoes and the latest fashions. You both meet up later and neither of you has found quite what you are looking for.

Now let's rewind the day. As you are both chatting over coffee, you mention you're looking for a new dress. Your friend asks what it's for and if you have got something specific in mind. You explain that it's a summer party and you have an idea you are looking for a yellow dress with white polka dots and a white collar. You carry on by asking your friend what the shoes are for and if she has got something in mind. She is looking for some leopard-print heels with about a two-inch heel to go with an outfit for Saturday night.

You both leave each other and head for the shops. Your friend is walking past a window and her eyes are drawn to a yellow dress with white spots and a white collar; she immediately texts you and tells you where it is. Your friend would never have noticed that dress if you hadn't explained to her exactly what you wanted.

Whenever I mention to anyone about flamingos being my lucky sign, they immediately begin seeing them. I'm always getting photos of flamingos and even being bought all kinds of flamingo-themed gifts. Getting clear on the 'what' means we can activate others' minds to help us find what we are looking for.

So if I was to mention here now that I would love to meet Lorraine Kelly, you'd remember that, right? And if you knew a way to help make this a reality, you might want to contact me to help me achieve one of my goals… OK, I'll leave that one with you, ha ha.

Inviting others in is very much about deciding who you need right now, where that tribe or person hangs out, and finding them. It's finding the people you need in your life right now for a reason. The relationship you form may last a season or potentially a lifetime. We don't know that yet, we just know the reason right now.

It's interesting how, when we need people the most, we are often less likely to feel it's the right time to ask or invite them in.

No is not offensive

It was 9 p.m. on a frosty Sunday evening and I was standing in the taxi rank at Manchester Piccadilly station. I was thankful that I had left the heating on at home and the house would be warm and welcoming. Standing there, I was drawn to a homeless person who was methodically approaching everyone in the freezing taxi queue. The queue during the last five to ten minutes had a rolling average of 20 people. The man approached each person in turn and asked if they could spare any change. He was polite and responded to those that gave and those that said no with the same thank you and nod of his head. He didn't take offence when anyone said no; he simply moved on. The response he received was impressive; a couple of people would say no and the others said yes. No one seemed offended that he had asked, whether they opted to give or not.

Each of us will have a different thought running through our heads when approached by a homeless person asking us directly for money. What impressed me, however, was that this man was taking action. He knew what he wanted: money. He saw a group of people who could potentially provide him with what he wanted and so, quite simply, he asked for it.

It was a perfect example of a very simple lesson: ask for what you want and if someone can't or won't give it to you, they will say no and that's OK. Look for the next person who can or will. There will always be someone further down the line who will say yes. That evening, for every two no's the homeless man received, he received one yes.

He came from a place of love, assuming someone would say yes. If he had approached them from a place of fear, he would never have asked in the first place. He would have been too afraid of the word no. For this guy, his fear of hunger was much greater than his fear of rejection.

If the ratio was this high when you went after what you want in life, you would be racing around asking people as quickly as possible, knowing that every time you received two no's, a yes would be coming next. I love the simplicity of this. Some will say no, some will say yes, but we won't know what the ratio is unless we ask. Many people will never work out their ratio of how many no's they need to get a yes, because when they hear their first no they give up.

In effect we reject ourselves before we even give anyone else the opportunity to reject us. We imagine people will say no and give ourselves all kinds of negative self-talk about why someone will say no: we aren't good enough, or we may offend people by asking for help, support, ideas, time. If we can get used to the fact that some will say yes and some will say no or not right now, we know we have a 50:50 chance of getting what we want.

Just keep asking

Jack Canfield, my mentor, wrote the first *Chicken Soup for the Soul* book along with Mark Victor Hansen. They thought the book was fabulous, sent it off to a publisher and received their first no, then another, then another. They received over 140 no's from publishers for a book that went on to sell over ten million copies in its first edition. Over 500 million books were subsequently sold worldwide. It's an incredible book that touches hearts – 500 million hearts that would never have been touched if they had accepted the first no.

Never give up

I first met Michelle four years ago, when she was 33. At the time, she was working in the legal department of a large organisation. Michelle shared her goal with me – in fact, she shared it with everyone – she wanted to secure a training contract to qualify as a solicitor. I loved Michelle. She had great energy and as I got to know her more, I learnt more about her back story.

Michelle had grown up in a far from supportive family. Her parents didn't work and as soon as she was old enough, they thought she should be supporting herself. She left home at 17, having quit school the year before with no qualifications. When she left home, she got a job in an office in Manchester and worked doing the same thing day in, day out, until finally, one day, she thought there must be another way – there must be more to life. Michelle is super bright, but because of a lack of encouragement in her earlier years she didn't recognise this in herself.

She began looking around at courses, found two legal secretary courses and applied. She completed the course and managed to get a job as a legal secretary, working at this for six years. During this time she had her baby daughter, Grace, but whilst on maternity leave she was made redundant.

She knew she wanted more for her daughter and for their life together and decided to gain further qualifications. She made a huge decision to apply for university. The recession had hit and jobs were scarce. Michelle wanted to be sure she was securing a future for her new family and, having had a taste of the legal profession, decided to take the risk of attempting to become a solicitor. When she shared this with her parents, their response was 'that will never happen'. Michelle ignored them and took a part-time job on the fish counter in a supermarket. At 28, she went to university and completed a degree in law and practice, leaving with a commendation.

Next came the challenge of finding a supervised position with a solicitor, a coveted training contract – the final stage before becoming a solicitor in her own right. Training contracts are hard to come by and Michelle wasn't the typical trainee. She started sending CVs and receiving rejections. This didn't deter Michelle, who had been told no all her life; a no or discouragement only made her stronger.

She went through every law firm listed on the internet in Manchester and applied to them all. She even went to an event for legal professionals and stood up in the middle of the packed room, addressed everyone, introduced herself and asked for help in finding a contract. Close to two years later and with hundreds of CVs already dispatched, Michelle finally secured her training contract. In a few short months, she will celebrate becoming a fully fledged solicitor.

Michelle said, 'I'm in,' and she was staying in until she got what she wanted. *No is not an offensive word; it's a step on the journey to finding your yes.*

Who or what do you need right now?

'Who or what do you need right now?' This is a question I regularly ask myself if I'm a little stuck with something, and I ask clients too. This question takes your mind out of any current challenge and seeks to find an answer to a different question; when we have the answer to this question, we can seek the answer to our problem.

One client answered the question with the words 'a mentor'. She was a newly appointed CEO, which can be a lonely place. When you reach the top, it's a good idea to connect with other people who have been there and understand your world. I asked her who she would choose, if she could have anyone. She said she would love someone like Karren Brady. Karren Brady is a super successful businesswoman who is more in the public eye now because of her role on the TV show *The Apprentice*. My client reached out and asked Karren if she would be interested in mentoring her. Would you reach out to someone you don't know at all and ask for help? It's a brave step. In this case it paid off and Karren agreed to meet. That is pretty amazing, isn't it? A woman who must have a million plates spinning said yes when asked for help.

Exercise

Who or what do I need right now to help me get where I want to be? Consider your goals or something you are stuck with and could do with some advice on. Who has done it before? Don't limit yourself to people you already know. Write a list, be brave and call.

Summary of the I of the LIPSTICK principles – Inviting Others In

- Find your tribe; join a membership or network that can help you.
- Ask for help; if people have the capacity, most want to help.

- Never be afraid of the word 'no'. There is always a yes out there.
- Come from a place of love and trust that there are people who want to help.
- Life is not a solo sport; you do not have to be alone and do it all yourself.
- New mantra: 'Between me and my goals are two things... time and action.'

CONFIDENCE

Confidence from a place of love:

Feeling confident leads to a life of freedom, a life of feeling connected to other people in an honest and meaningful way. Confidence enables a life of opportunity and experiences, friendships, romances and travel. A life of saying yes – a life of knowing you're doing what you're supposed to be doing and that you are exactly where you're supposed to be.

Confidence from a place of fear:

Lack of confidence or low self-esteem is a barrier not just to people but also to possibilities, to dreams, to opportunities of laughter, to feeling invincible, to feeling on top of the world. It prevents relationships from flourishing or even starting. It stops great ideas coming to fruition; it stops openness and honest relationships; it stops potential being reached and businesses starting. Low self-esteem can negatively impact health and the way you show up in the world.

Our next LIPSTICK principle is C for Confidence. In this chapter you will learn how to change your thinking to build confidence, and how you are in control. You will learn how to look beyond events to gain confidence and how to use your body or an alter ego to try confidence on.

When it comes to confidence, it's easy to look around and think everyone else has that coveted confidence, and they are rocking it. This is actually far from the truth. In reality those people are very probably looking back at you and thinking the same thing, that you have the magic wand for confidence.

In seminars I'll ask people to introduce themselves to the person next to them and have a chat before we begin talking about confidence. When we start to talk about confidence, I'll ask everyone to give themselves a score between 1 and 10 on how confident they see themselves. Then, before they have a chance to share their score, I ask them to ask the person next to them what score they would give them and some reasons why. Without fail, 95% of those in the room have been scored considerably higher by the person they just met than they have scored themselves. The reasons people give for someone appearing confident include their openness to chat, their smile, the way they stand, even the clothes they wear.

I hear from so many people who would love to have more confidence because they know their lack of it is holding them back. We ultimately have one shot at life and it's terrifying to think we might get to the end and think: 'S**t! I know I didn't enjoy it as much as I could. I know I didn't do everything I could have done. I know I could have done more... if only.' It's an awful thought that you could prevent yourself from achieving your full potential because of a lack of confidence.

When I speak on confidence, the talks are always full so I know it's something lots of people want more of, and yet everyone who walks through the door looks confident.

What is confidence? I'm not sure confidence really is a thing, it's more of a *not thing*. When I first started speaking in front of audiences, I was very nervous. I would worry about messing up, worry about what people would think of me, worry about getting it wrong and making an idiot of myself. All those what ifs – WHIFs.

With practice some of the WHIF thoughts began to disappear. They weren't replaced with anything. It wasn't that I suddenly felt confident, it was that I wasn't worrying; it was a calm place rather than an energy-fuelled feeling. It's simply a place where your head is clear of WHIFs. So in this chapter I'll share more on raising your self-esteem and losing self-doubt so you can arrive at the peaceful place of feeling confident.

I mentioned public speaking above as it is a great example for confidence. Apparently, on the list of fears people have, public speaking is number two after spiders and higher up the list than death. Would people really rather die than speak in front of a crowd? No, but the thought of speaking in front of people fills many with dread, and their minds fill with all the WHIF's that come from speaking in front of people.

These are the same thoughts that can fill our heads when meeting people for the first time or putting ideas forward at work. We start to worry about how we will come across and what people will think about us. The biggest lesson in life to learn is that we can never, ever know or control what people think about us (unless they tell us). Thinking that other people could feel negatively about us is fear-based thinking. It's coming directly from a place of fear and will hold us back from being our best self. Conversely, thinking the opposite and coming from a place of love will turn our outlook upside down and sky-rocket our self-esteem and confidence.

Imagine for a moment that all the people in your world – your family, friends, colleagues, strangers – want what's best for you; they are all there silently cheering you on and encouraging you the whole time. With this support and knowledge would we take more risks, speak out more, try more and put ourselves forward more?

Let's be honest, we will never know what people are thinking of us and indeed if they are thinking about us at all.

In your twenties you spend your time
worrying what *others* think
In your thirties you spend your time
worrying what *you* think
In your forties you *give up* worrying what *others* think
*In your fifties you realise no one was ever thinking about
you anyway – they were worrying about themselves!*

We have two choices when we think about what others
think of us – actually, make that three:

1. Don't care and realise people aren't really giving
   that much time to thinking of us.
2. Believe everyone has your back, wants the best
   for us and loves us.
3. Believe everyone is against us and wants us to
   fall or fail.

Talk to yourself

A belief is quite simply a thought we have about how
things happen in our world. For example, while the
majority of the population believe the world is round,
I have listened to interviews with people on the radio
who are adamant that the world is flat; they completely
believe it and have gathered evidence to support this
belief. Although we might think we could change their
belief with other evidence that the world is round, we
would not be able to. They have their belief and that is
their prerogative.

Our own beliefs may be true at a certain time to us, but, and this is a big but, we don't have to hold onto the same belief for ever. We can change our thoughts and beliefs depending on what new information we have gained or how we have changed as a person. Did you believe in Santa Claus? Did you believe in the tooth fairy? Did you believe you would marry the first person you had a crush on? Did you believe the world might end when you had your heart broken for the first time? Some beliefs we just outgrow as they are no use to us any more.

Our beliefs, our thoughts, are either helping us feel good or holding us back. The good news is that beliefs we have about ourselves can be changed; we can grow out of them just like we did when we stopped believing in Santa Claus. You can change them and it's pretty easy with a little practice.

The key to this is noticing what you are telling yourself. Once you notice the negatives, you can change them. For example, 'I'll never find another job'; 'I'll never find love'; 'I'm terrible with money'; 'I could never run a marathon'; 'I look awful'... Any thought you have can be changed to support what you want. This is just you being in control, taking action making a change and then talking to yourself in the right way.

Take control and say no to any thoughts holding you back, any fear-based beliefs, and turn them round to being a thought coming from a place of love. It's time to become your own best friend and use the same encouragement and words of affirmation that you would for a best friend: 'You got this'; 'You can do it'; 'You look great'; 'There's an abundance of opportunity out there'; 'My perfect partner is out there somewhere'; 'I'm great with money'…

As you become more in tune with yourself and your thoughts, you will start to notice the thoughts that don't make you feel good or sound defeatist. You are letting go of worry and fear and saying yes to a life filled with love. When you catch yourself thinking a thought which doesn't make you feel good, or criticising yourself or saying you can't do something, put your hand on your heart and say: 'No, I see you, I see you, fear, and I can let you go. I believe in myself and I come from a place of love.'

Practise talking to yourself with the right messages: 'I am confident'; 'I feel great'. The more positive things you say to yourself, the more your self-esteem grows, and in time the negative thoughts just disappear.

Ask yourself what words of encouragement or support you most need to hear today. Then become your own cheerleader; write those words down and have them close by you – read them, read them and read them again.

The 'not confident' girl on the train

There's something about taking the train. You never know who you might end up chatting to and even if you don't chat to anyone, the hum of the train can be relaxing. Last summer, taking the train from Manchester to London, I was in for a treat as my companion for this journey turned out to be Erika, a lovely 24-year-old living in Manchester and working for a large media corporation. As we chatted about life, Erika shared that she wasn't completely happy in her role, had recently split from her boyfriend and felt she was somewhere we have all been – at a crossroads.

Erika enquired about why I was taking the trip to London, and I told her I had been booked as a 'Body Confidence Expert' and would be taking some women through exercises to help build self-esteem and confidence. Erika immediately said, 'Oh, I'd love to have confidence.' So, I asked her two questions:

1. How do you know you haven't got confidence?
2. If you had all the confidence in the world, no fear, what would you do?

Her response to question 1 was that she felt she held herself back, and she said she spent a lot of time worrying about whether to do things or not and talked herself out of things (with negative WHIFs).

Her list in answer to question 2 included:

- discussing a change of role with her manager
- asking for a pay rise
- joining a new fitness group
- making plans for the future
- dating again

This is a list which many of us will have created at some stage in our lives. Really, it is a list of things you want to do, or 'goals'.

A question for you, what would you do if you had no fear?

Exercise

This is a simple strategy for reducing nerves and becoming brave about something you really want to do but have been putting off is to utilise that wonderful imagination again. Imagine the thing you want to do, and fast forward in your mind to that moment in the future after you've just done it. Imagine it's all gone to plan and you feel good. Create the positive movie. You can't get nervous about something that's gone well. The thing you're actually nervous about is the fantasy fear movie where it doesn't go to plan; you're spending too much time on the negative WHIFs and no time on the 'what if it all goes perfectly?'. Remember this from LIPSTICK principle 2 – Imagine?

On the train Erika and I talked about the conversation she would have with her manager, and the more we discussed it, the less scary it became. I asked Erika to describe how she would feel after having the conversation with her manager. She said she'd feel good and at least she would know where she stood so she could make some decisions from there. The moment came when Erika realised she was completely capable of having that conversation, and she decided she was going to go for it.

When Erika left the train that day, her outlook had changed. She had a new view on what her next steps were about to be. I could see her becoming visibly excited. She was glowing as she recognised all these things were possible and she could actually do them. She felt in control.

But what had actually changed? In some ways nothing had changed, but then again everything had changed for Erika. Her doubt had gone and with that she had released the brakes on her life. She had gained clarity and a sense of purpose. She had had a moment of 'realisation' that this was all in her control. It wasn't that she hadn't got confidence; it was more that she hadn't been clear about what she really wanted and how much she wanted it.

For anyone who had sat next to Erika, who was a gorgeous girl, it would have been easy to look and make a judgement about a girl with a great job who had her whole life ahead of her was full of confidence. It turned out this was not the case; Erika was one of the 92% of women who have suffered from self-doubt.

Use an alter ego to build confidence

What would Mariella do?

My friend Charlotte and I went on holiday a couple of years ago. Charlotte, my lovely friend, had suggested I seek some sunshine a few months after Mum had passed away. I loved the idea of sunshine but wasn't sure I was up for a holiday; I didn't know quite what company I would be and didn't really want to be away from home. Charlotte said, 'We'll just go lie in the sun and have early nights. You don't need to go out, just come and have a rest.'

Charlotte was right; the rest was just what I needed. We went for four days. On the last night I suggested we go out. We had barely left the hotel really and I thought I should make the effort. Charlotte had been so kind and was happy to stay in and have low-key evenings every night. We went along to a bar in the town which people in the hotel had said would be busy. We arrived very early and the place was almost empty. It made me feel old being out before everything got going.

It was chilly and we had our jackets on. A few people began filtering in. We were sitting quite close to the bar, and a beautiful young woman in a stunning red dress (no jacket) was standing at the bar. As she turned around, I smiled and said, 'I love your dress.' She thanked me and we got chatting.

Her name was Mariella and she was in her twenties. Charlotte and I were in our forties. As we chatted to Mariella, she told us she was out to find a man. Mariella knew what she wanted and it was refreshing to hear her state quite clearly what she was there for. We were intrigued 'oldies' and asked how this would work. Charlotte and I then got a crash course in the latest apps for meeting people, the difference between what a man you might want to marry might look like compared to a man you wanted to date. Mariella was looking for a date that night. She was really fun, a confident young woman, and we had a good laugh hearing about the ins and outs of dating. She also tried to explain to us the exercises you needed to do to make your bum pert. It was very funny.

Next thing you know, Mariella said, 'That guy there would be a great date.' By now we were on tenterhooks – what was going to happen? 'Watch,' she said. If we'd blinked, we would have missed it. Mariella made a kind of circling motion with her toe as she looked over at this chap for just a second and then she continued to chat to us. Less than two minutes later the man came

over to say hello. He seemed nice. We soon lost Mariella
as the two got chatting.

That night Charlotte and I spent some time trying to figure
out what Mariella had done, and there was much foot
swirling going on between us. We never quite perfected
it. The following morning we had such a laugh and we
created a new phrase: 'What would Mariella do?'

Mariella knew what she wanted. She looked confident
and had an air about her. After that, if ever Charlotte
and I went out with the idea that we might end up
talking to men, we laughed and would say, 'What
would Mariella do?' Just thinking about it made us
stand differently, walk taller and feel braver – rather
like having an alter ego to step into.

Try it on

A super quick way to create confidence in yourself is to
step into the zone and try on the persona of someone
you think is confident. Stand like they stand. Walk like
they walk (and twizzle your foot like they do… ha ha
ha). If you can just step into that persona and try it on,
your body instantly sends messages to your brain that
you are confident, and then the feedback loop sets in:
brain tells body… body tells brain and, voilà, you're
'doing confidence'! Consider how confident people
walk, stand, hold their heads, their posture, smile,
and then try copying their behaviour. Honestly, it

works wonders, especially for those times you really need it, such as walking into a packed meeting room, presenting in front of colleagues, walking into a bar.

When Paula was being put forward for director in the firm she worked for, we discussed at length what was involved in the process, what would be different in the role, and what she needed in order to step up to it. Paula said she would need more confidence. I enquired as to what having more confidence would mean and how she would be different at director level. Paula's view was that directors interact with people in the office more, that they seem to have a bit more time for people. They take a real interest in what everyone in the office is doing. As we chatted about this, I asked if there was any reason Paula couldn't act in that way now, i.e. take time for everyone and show a real interest in what everyone was doing.

There is nothing stopping you behaving the way you think you would act if you had more confidence or got that promotion. Trying on these behaviours will build your confidence and, before you know it, you're not trying it on any more, you're doing it.

You *can* raise your self-esteem and build your confidence; you just have to do it consciously. It's a bit like going to the gym. On the first day you do five minutes' exercise and you already feel tired. Then gradually you build your strength and, pretty soon, you can do an hour of exercise no problem. Trying out the different behaviours feels weird at first but soon they will become a habit and you won't remember what it was like before.

Confidence and self-esteem need deliberate exercise; the more you build them, the more they grow and the better you feel. You can practise feeling confident just as you can practise baking a cake or learning a sport. The more you practise, the more skilled you become, until one day you notice this has become a natural way of being for you. You are confident, happy and comfortable, proud of who you are.

Summary of the C of the LIPSTICK principles – Confidence

- You can change your beliefs if you've outgrown them and you make a determined effort to let go and welcome new beliefs in.
- You are in control.
- You can make a list of things you would do if you had more confidence; these become goals.
- To let go of nerves and fear, utilise your mind movies and create the movie where it all goes right.
- Try out the body language and behaviour of someone who you believe has confidence.
- New mantra: 'What would Mariella do?'

KEEP IT SIMPLE (SWEETHEART) – KISS

KISS from a place of love:

KISS from a place of love is getting up each morning and having a sense of excitement about what the day has in store for you. It is taking a moment to think about people in your life and sending them love; it is creating love in you by appreciating everything you have currently and having an optimistic feeling about your future. It is looking in the mirror and seeing a wonderful, happy person with spirit, energy and focus looking back at you. Feel good about who you are and what you do; feel proud of your progress. Feel connected to people, with a commitment to share the love every day and shine light on others. This is KISS from a place of love.

KISS from a place of fear:

KISS from a place of fear is getting up each morning and having a sense of dread about what the day has in store for you looking at yourself in the mirror and making some kind of criticism of yourself and looking at other people you know and thinking they have it all and you don't. It is criticising and complaining about the people around you or your circumstances, feeling alone and empty.

Keep It Simple (Sweetheart) – KISS is our final chapter of *The LIPSTICK Principles,* and I have saved the best for last. This principle is all about you and learning to love yourself, love your life and love everyone in it. This principle is like part of your five a day; think of everything in this chapter as your mental first aid kit for feeling good about you. You will learn how to introduce and adopt love for life into your daily routine, and how to feel proud of yourself and connect with your positivity; you will learn how to spread the love and make other people's day; you will learn how to nourish your soul and feel proud of yourself every day.

This is quite a personal chapter because I adopted every one of the strategies when I made the decision to adopt 'come from a place of love not fear' as my core guiding principle in life. These are the strategies that reset me after Mum died and have kept me strong and full of love and joy since.

If you connected with this book hoping for a magic wand to transform your life, this principle contains the magic you have been looking for – easy-to-implement strategies that will change your world and how you feel in it. My guess is that you will have read the book and thought it all sounds like quite a good idea, and that the strategies you have learnt so far are strategies you will utilise in the future. You have already learnt so much but you may be thinking, 'OK, where do I start taking action?' Right here, this is the chapter where you start; these are the strategies you start with to get yourself to a place where you feel brilliant these strategies you implement every day.

We have 50,000 thoughts a day; let's layer them with thoughts coming from a place of love, let go of worry and fear and love life.

When I ask people what they really want, it usually comes down to one thing: to be happy. Can you be happy without achieving every goal you ever set? Can you be happy without being in a loving relationship or owning the biggest house? Of course you can. Material objects, money, houses and so on may help us feel happy if we've worked for them and feel very proud of what we have achieved. However, I have never found any correlation between having things and *being* consistently happy. I've worked with women at both ends of the wealth scale and whether the bank account is large or small, the shared goal is always the same: to feel happy, to feel love and to be loved. Remember the bank account we all have in common is the most valuable of all, the bank account of time, and the goal is that our time is filled with love and joy.

Conversely, although the goal is often love, what I also notice is just how many barriers and walls we can create to stop love getting in, and I don't just mean love in terms of a relationship. I mean basic love of ourselves – which is why we are so reluctant to accept compliments and praise. I mean truly loving ourselves by not beating ourselves up or criticising ourselves. We even create barriers to loving ourselves.

Why? Because of fear – fear of being hurt, or looking stupid, or failing. Protecting ourselves from hurt or failure comes in many forms. It can come in the form of saying no to an invitation or a date, or not sharing what we really think and feel with others because we don't want to open ourselves up to hurt. Or it can come in the form of doubt, or not trying new techniques to make us happy because they may not work for us.

The challenge with protecting ourselves from pain in the form of hurt, rejection or embarrassment is this: we may be attempting to protect ourselves from the negative but at the same time we are actually creating huge barriers that separate us from the things we really want: love and happiness. You cannot experience life full out or love full out if at the back of your mind, you're worried about failure or hurt. It's impossible. This is why the core guiding principle of coming from a place of love not fear is so important, because coming from love there is no fear and you can experience life as you were intended to.

We are all born with the same opportunity to let love in. As we are born, the midwife doesn't take a look and say, 'Oh, this one here will protect themselves' or 'This one is going to go for it'. Life's experiences and how we respond to them are what change our ability to love ourselves and let love in.

I mentioned in LIPSTICK principle 1 – Life lessons – how, many years ago, I came out of a six-year relationship that had done very little for my confidence. I was upset and frustrated with myself for sticking for such a long time with something that wasn't working, hoping it would get better. When I left that relationship, I made a decision that I wouldn't do that again and repeatedly said to myself, 'I'm not doing that again.' I said it over and over; I wanted to let myself know I would protect myself in the future from hurt, pain and humiliation. What I didn't know then was that, in repeating that statement over and over, 'I won't do that again, I won't be in a relationship like that again', I was putting a blanket of protection around myself because I didn't want to feel that way ever again.

Our deep unconscious, our soul, is always listening. It listens and does everything it can to help us achieve what we want, whatever our goal. In this case, what I was telling myself was that I didn't want a relationship again, so my soul helped me create an unconscious fear of relationships. It sounds ridiculous but when we make a decision and create a belief, it becomes very deep rooted even if we aren't consciously thinking of it all the time. That's why talking to yourself positively is crucial. The result for me was close to five years in my twenties of being single, protecting myself from hurt but ultimately also protecting myself from experiencing love with a partner. Even when I consciously thought it would be nice to meet someone, the unconscious kicked in.

My friends love reminding me of the times I'd meet great guys and then, after two or three dates with all going well, I would freak and end it all with no explanation. Even I didn't understand why. I remember once a lovely guy I'd met was coming to visit me for the weekend and I actually started hyperventilating as I was in such a state of fear. I had to call and cancel. The poor guy had already been travelling for three hours and must have thought I was crazy, and I was – crazy with fear.

Some 20 years later, just a couple of months after making the decision to come from a place of love not fear, I randomly met someone I'd met back then when I was frightened of relationships, and it turned out he was the love of my life – 20 years later!

This book is not about finding love with a partner; it's about finding love for ourselves and our lives, and everyone around us. (But if you are looking for romantic love, then following the strategies in this chapter will certainly help you find love for yourself, let go of fear and let love in so that when it comes you know you deserve it and you're ready to jump off the cliff without the parachute and say, 'I'm in.')

Let's take off the blanket of protection and let love in.

Let love in – a love rampage

A few years ago I learnt that if you show appreciation for what you currently have in your world, you will feel better about yourself and attract more of what you love to you. If you adopt an attitude of gratitude, it will help remind you that there are great things here already and you have a lot to be grateful for.

Initially I tried to express appreciation for what I had in my life by operating an *attitude of gratitude three times a day*: I am grateful for a roof over my head, I am grateful for my family, I am grateful for my job... that kind of thing. Every day after Mum passed away I continued the attitude of gratitude, thinking of three things each day I was grateful for. I stuck to it. I was grateful I was still breathing, and that my Dad, family and friends were around me.

One day I noticed myself experiencing a feeling that had been missing for a while. When you lose someone, you go through the motions of life a little; you're doing it but you're not really feeling it. On this day, in a fleeting moment, I noticed a feeling – a feeling of happiness. I was over the moon: 'Oh wow, that was a genuine feeling of happy.' It was like an awakening, and as I noticed this feeling, I loved it. I said out loud, 'I love that I felt that way, I love that I can feel happy.'

I decided to go on a love rampage. I loved the fact that I'd even said the word 'love' out loud. A love rampage meant rather radically changing my approach to appreciation and ramping things right up. Rather than just saying out loud the things I appreciated three times a day, I began saying the words 'I love' a lot. I wanted to be filled with love not just gratitude.

I began using the word 'love' in front of more or less everything: I love that I have hot water for a shower, I love the handles on my wardrobes, I love honey on my toast, I love my garden, I love my house, I love Manchester, I love that my friend called today. Waking up in the morning and saying, 'I love this bed', 'I love my Dad', 'I love that the sun is shining', and then continuing it all day radically changed how I approached and felt about my life.

Very quickly I noticed a huge difference in how I was feeling – a feeling of love and joy constantly, as if I was being wrapped in a cocoon of love. I felt joyful, with a spring in my step, and had a whole new experience of hope and excitement about the future, while living in the moment. This feeling of joy remained and actually grew; I felt love and happy.

Neuroscience has shown that regularly expressing gratitude literally changes the molecular structure of the brain. When we experience the feeling of being happy, the nervous system is affected and we are more peaceful, calm and less reactive. In a study on the impact of showing gratitude, by Robert A. Eammons, Professor of Psychology, participants in the group that expressed gratitude felt 25% better than those not expressing gratitude, and another bonus was that they reported 1.5 hours more exercise per week – so being grateful could get you fitter!

No wonder I was feeling great on the love rampage; saying 'I love' about things you have in your life is gratitude ramped up.

19 'I loves'

Some days I was saying the words 'I love' over a hundred times. To share this technique with others I created an optimal amount of 'I loves' to say each day. To integrate this technique into your life, the magic number is **19**, and later I'll share in more detail how it works out to be this number and how to use your 'I loves'. But don't be restricted by this – go for your life on your love rampage.

One day I was walking down the street and hopping on and off the pavement as I overtook pedestrians on my way to a meeting. It was a warm sunny day and Manchester looked glorious. Everyone seemed to be smiling, as they do on sunny days. As I was hopping on and off the pavement, my mind went back to the year before, when I'd had surgery on my leg and was not able to walk for three months. I suddenly recognised that here I was hopping on and off the pavement and that 'hey, I love walking', and then I realised 'wow, I can speak too' (I've never had a problem with that before but there are people who have lost the ability to speak), so I was happy to say that I loved that I could speak. When you get in the swing with a love rampage, you soon get to a place where you love just everything.

Recently some friends and I were on holiday in Tenerife (quite a windy island) and one friend said, 'It's so windy, it's just far too windy.' To be fair, this was as they went to retrieve their book which had flown off the table for the third time. I sat and felt the wind on my face. As I did so, I thought of another friend who had been admitted to hospital that week, and I pictured her holed up in a stuffy, sterile room; I knew she would be wishing she could feel a breeze on her face. This reminded me of how lucky we are if we can feel the wind, rain or sunshine on our face, how lucky we are to experience the weather, and I made my statement: 'I love the wind.'

The love rampage also becomes a benefit when it comes to mindfulness and being present. Whilst you're in the present and looking around and noticing all the things you love – the sunshine, the blue sky, the leaves on the trees – you are also being present and focusing on the now, so it's a double bonus.

It's pretty tough to be worrying about a report for work or what's for tea when you are in that moment filling your life with love. But you can blend these thoughts into your love rampage. It changes your thinking when you say, 'I love that I have a report to finish for work' or 'I love that I have tea to make for people I love tonight'. It's also pretty difficult to think about what's wrong in your world when you are filling your mind and nourishing your soul by reiterating what you love about life.

The clients who implement this strategy often feel awkward at first, but it is astonishing how quickly they gain a new perspective and feel the love. Jackie had been feeling a bit disconnected from life and felt she was constantly on the go, unable to stop and consider where she was or where she was heading. Her husband was busy too, and life seemed to be a constant conversation about who was picking the kids up when, where the kids needed to be, and every day ended with them sitting down exhausted for a subdued evening meal, closely followed by sleep. When life gets busy, it's easy to forget why you're doing what you're doing and negativity can creep in. My first step with any coaching is always to help people get back to feeling good, so I gave Jackie the task of 19 'I loves' every day.

Jackie decided to share this home work with her family and get everyone involved; who wouldn't benefit from having their love tank filled? A few days later I asked Jackie how she was getting on and how she was feeling. 'Great,' she said. 'I feel amazing. The sun was shining this weekend and I don't know if it's the love rampage but I just noticed how much there is to love; the sky is blue, the fields are green, I love it.'

She also shared that the love rampage had created a new energy in their house, which focused on love. She said that it was helping her daughters (aged 10 and 13) to see life through a beautiful loving lens. The kids embraced it and thought it was great fun. At dinner each evening they began asking what Mummy had loved today and what Daddy had loved. Dinner time became a beautiful moment of reflection on what had been brilliant that day, which is such a powerful exercise at the close of a day.

If I was your coach, I'd always start any meeting with the question: what has been the best thing that's happened to you this week? It's a question that helps people recognise what's been good and focuses the mind on the positives. However, it doesn't always work immediately, because there are times when I ask this question and people just can't come up with anything (which is sad to hear). When life gets really busy, people don't take time to reflect back on the great things that happen each day. When you start the love rampage, it clears your mind and focuses on the positives, and it's such a quick turnaround; literally within a few days you feel different.

The beautiful hidden secret in the love rampage is that although you're often directing your 'I love' statements at other people or things around you, your soul is always listening, and your soul feels the love.

Think about what someone look like who's full of love... You can see it, can't you? If you have a friend who's recently met someone and is in love, or perhaps has just got a promotion, they look different. When you fill yourself with love, you look different, you feel different.

We need to fill our love tanks and keep them filled all day.

I've broken the love rampage down into themes to help you focus. Before long you won't need a guide; it will all become second nature. You will be so full of love that it will come naturally.

- Say five times 'I love' about people.
- Say five times 'I love' about things.
- Say five times 'I love' about things people do.

When you are saying 'I love' about people, although it's lovely if you say it to the person concerned, you can also just say it out loud to yourself. Every morning I wake up and say 'I love you' to my Dad, who lives miles away, and I say 'I love you' to my Mum and spend a moment thinking of people and saying 'I love you'. The people I'm saying it about don't need to be with me or in the same room; we can think of them and send them love wherever they are.

But that's only fifteen 'I loves' – what about the other four? The final four are for the most special person in your world – you! We save the best for last, as it's then time to spread the love to yourself. Yes, at the end of every day it's time to utilise your final four 'I loves' on yourself.

This is really about connecting with yourself, loving yourself again and seeing you. I want to get the message deeply set in your soul that you love and back yourself.

Mirror mirror

Warning: This will be a game changer for you. It will feel very, very weird to start with. When you first do this, you may experience nerves (good fear); you may even want to laugh or cry. So although you may feel daft, remember that's only how it will feel at first.

This is a ritual to start and never stop. It is you reconnecting with your beautiful soul, backing yourself and beginning to fall in love with you again. When was the last time you told yourself that you loved you?

Add this ritual to your daily routine. When you have brushed your teeth in the evening (or morning) and you're in the bathroom in front of the mirror (probably best to be alone!), look in the mirror, look yourself straight in the eye and say, 'I love you,' pause and then say it again. Keep the eye contact up, pause and say it again, 'I love you.' Even better, add your name to the end of the phrase: 'I love you, Amanda', 'I love you, Jackie'.

Here's a challenge for you: try this for 21 days consecutively to start with. Just see how it goes. Expect it to feel strange, maybe even daft and emotional for the first few days, and then see what happens. Begin to notice if it feels different and what changes for you.

One lady shared with me that she had always avoided looking at herself in the mirror and hated having photos taken. The idea of a selfie was bad enough, never mind looking in the mirror and saying 'I love you'. She was a successful lawyer, confident on the outside but on the inside she didn't feel the same. This exercise didn't feel good and was way outside her comfort zone. She tried it and didn't like it and wanted to give up. But she also realised that she wanted to feel good. She was doing really well at work and she wanted to feel like she was doing well; she wanted to learn to love who she was. She persisted, even though she cringed every night for the first week. Then something changed and she got used to it; she said she didn't necessarily feel good about doing it but she would continue. It was a few more weeks before she admitted that this nightly routine of connecting with herself, giving herself love, was having an impact. She'd started to laugh and smile when she said it, and most of all to believe it: 'When I say it, Amanda, I think I actually mean it now.'

When we are looking to let love in, let's start with you; you are the important one here.

Your Best Friend
You have a friend the best there is
She loves you like no other
She has a complete love for you
As unconditional as a mother
She wants to see you laugh and smile
She wants to see you rest awhile
She wants to see you dream big dreams
And get excited about hare-brained schemes
She wants to see you feel the love
And greet everyone with a hug
She believes in you when times are tough
She wants you to know you are enough
If you're curious who this could be
You simply say 'Ah that friend is me'
Amanda Brown

For you to notice the benefits of some of these strategies, it would be good for you to know where you are now so you can check back in with how you feel once you start implementing them. In coaching sessions and seminars I'll ask the question: if you were to give yourself a score right now between 1 and 10 of how high your self-esteem is today, what would it be? Self-esteem is how we feel about ourselves, confidence, self-respect, happiness.

So before you start implementing all the strategies and going on your love rampage, check in with yourself and decide on a number between 1 and 10 for how happy you are and where you are in terms of self-esteem (1 is low, 10 is high). If you are going to make these strategies part of your life, you will need to remember what they have done for you, because once you feel great it's pretty easy to forget when you didn't.

My number before I started on letting love in is......
Date...............

After taking up this strategy of the love rampage, I'd expect you to notice a change quite quickly as it's so powerful. If things don't feel that different, you could ramp up the love rampage to get you started. Remember I began with over a hundred, and 19 is a great number to maintain the feeling. These days I rarely count; it has become part of me and it will you too. Everything new just requires a little focus and practice to start with; you will soon be in the swing.

After 21 days you can come back and re-score yourself (mark the date on your calendar or in your phone).

> My number for how I feel in terms of happiness and self-esteem is...... Date...................

What feels different? What have you noticed?

Share the love

'Share the love' is one of my mantras in life, and part of your love rampage. Five of the 'I loves' in the love rampage are saved for other people and five more for the things people do. This is an important part of our love rampage and is a reflection of how we appreciate the people in our world – plus, in filling our own love tank, we also get to fill others' tanks and help them see they are fabulous too, #sharethelove.

I'd like to share with you how I ended up adopting this mantra. I was at a festival watching a band called the Cuban Brothers. I've seen them at many festivals over the years; they're a fun folk and soul band. When they play, the sun is usually shining and the lead singer likes to engage a happy crowd with banter and his philosophical views on life. He always ends his set with his philosophy on how to lead a good life, and this year he suggested we abide by these three rules to lead a good life:

1. Give more hugs.
2. Share the love.
3. Don't be a dick.

Cool rules for life, eh!

The festival where I heard these rules we had actually attended with a special occasion in mind. Historically this festival had an inflatable church as one of the attractions, and couples could share a ceremony at this church as a bit of fun. I'd seen the ceremonies over the years and always wanted to do it. This was my partner's first festival, and he said he would be happy to participate. On arrival at the festival we went to find the church to book the event. I was really disappointed to discover the church wasn't there this year, despite being on the website! Fascinating… not frustrating, ha ha… fascinating!

My friends, seeing my disappointment, took matters into their own hands and refused to be defeated; they wanted us to have a ceremony. What they did was incredible; they created a virtual wedding ceremony for us out of nowhere. One minute we had a camping area and an hour later we had an aisle, petals, a play-acting vicar, a number of speeches and a ceremony. It was really incredible fun and very moving. The 'best man' wrote his speech in an hour, and its conclusion included words of advice for the groom that were taken straight from the performance of the Cuban Brothers. For a long and happy marriage you need to follow three simple rules:

Share the love.
Give tons of hugs.
Don't be a dick.

(Coincidentally, I had always had a festival wedding on my vision board; I hadn't imagined it would look like this though.)

So these rules have become a kind of mantra in our lives and at least I have some nice words to use, should my partner ever 'act like a dick'.

Sharing the love is part of your love rampage. For a more work-oriented approach to a love rampage, you may think of it as creating a great culture and taking the time to value the great work others do, to appreciate the people you work with, lead by example, boost others' confidence or simply help raise other people's self-esteem. It's a moment to stop and notice the great work that's happening around you, and just as much as we need it, others do too. We can be the change.

You can make someone's day by sharing the love and showing appreciation by noticing what they do. If you're talking to a friend or family member, it's good to say, 'Thanks, I loved the dinner you cooked' or 'I love the way you listen and support me'. In a work environment, if the word love doesn't feel quite right, find other words: 'I really appreciate the help you gave me', 'I thought your presentation was fantastic', 'The way you handled that was brilliant', 'I love your cups of tea'...

I worked with Jo, a company director, who was seeking coaching as she had started in a new position and the work load was enormous. She found she was feeling exhausted and a bit stressed and overwhelmed, and she didn't think she was getting the right connection with her team. She wanted to be a good leader and do a great job and needed some time out to consider what that looked like and the best approach. She really needed some time to breathe and plan and reconnect with herself. With anyone who is experiencing stress and feeling overwhelmed, I start by connecting them back with themselves and building their love and energy back up.

In Jo's case I began with the simple love rampage, to help her connect back in with why she loved her role, her life and herself. In week one of the love rampage, Jo was in a meeting with five people from her team. She hadn't had much time to spend with them recently as she was always rushing from one meeting to another. During the meeting she invited everyone in her team to report back on the part of the project on which they were working. She started the meeting with a new question: what's the best thing that has happened to you this week? Everyone shared something that had gone well for them and enjoyed sharing a success. Jo remembered to be present in the meeting with her sole focus on listening to everyone. When they had each presented, she selected a couple of points for each team member and told them how much she loved the work they had done. At the end of the meeting she concluded with: 'Great work, brilliant, I love it.'

One female member of the team lingered after the meeting and, as Jo was leaving, she thanked her and explained she had been really nervous and was touched by the words of encouragement. Jo in that moment asked her colleague, 'Would you like a hug?!' The lady said that would be great and they had a quick hug. (I am an advocate of hugging in the right circumstances, but that's not always going to be the case at work. Here it worked perfectly and I have more to say later on hugs for nourishing the soul. Remember the rules for a happy life from the Cuban Brothers!)

Over the next couple of days Jo continued consciously to support her team and point out what they were doing that she loved. At the end of the week the woman she had hugged came to her and said, 'Have you got a minute?' She went on to tell Jo that outside of work she was having a few challenges. She had also been feeling a bit lost at work and had wondered if she was still on track. She'd felt disconnected and had even been considering if this was the right business for her. She was very open and then told Jo that this week she had felt completely different. She felt part of something, she felt valued and had her 'bounce' back. 'I think it started with that hug,' she said.

Sharing the love by helping others see their brilliance, and reinforce their great traits, leads to us being surrounded by happy people with confidence, and so the loop continues. We never know what a difference we make, or what is happening for people in their own world, but we should always remember that people might forget what you said, but they will never forget how you made them feel.

Recently I stayed at a hotel in Barcelona. When we first walked in we met Josefina, whose job it was to check us in. She did so much more than that. She had the most brilliant smile and welcomed us properly, showing real interest in our trip. She simply couldn't do enough for us. We were celebrating a birthday and she was so keen to make it special for us. One of the activities we wanted to undertake was to hire a Vespa and ride around the city. Josefina helped get it all arranged and was genuinely excited about our experience.

At the Vespa shop we bought a little keyring and on the evening we left I wrote a postcard for her saying how much we had loved our trip and, more to the point, how we had loved seeing her smile each day and loved her warm welcome. When we gave Josefina our thanks and the keyring, she burst into tears, came right around the check-in desk and hugged both of us. Josefina spread the love to us, and we appreciated it so much.

We have created some 'share the love cards' which you can give to someone to show that you appreciate them. Check them out on the website www. thelipstickprinciples.co.uk.

Sharing the love with others, praising others, noticing their great points and appreciating them is a 'win win'. It makes them feel good and reinforces what they do brilliantly. It's actually not very often people see what you see (remember everyone wants more confidence) so it's great to point out if you see something great in someone; the smallest thing makes all the difference. It's also a win for you because every time you see something good in someone else, it naturally reflects back at you; you feel good and notice some great ways of doing things you just might adopt.

We can make the difference and make someone's day.

WINning strategy

This next strategy is super powerful and forms part of your five a day happy tool kit. It's called the WINning strategy because when you implement it, you soon start to feel like you are winning.

You have learnt about the love rampage and how using the positive language of love 19 times a day raises your feelings of love and appreciation for yourself, your life and the people in it. For this strategy we return to the concept of your being your own best friend, but now you are entering into the arena of becoming your own coach on a daily basis.

This strategy is used in the evening at the end of the day. It can be done alone or you could get your family or partner involved. It evokes positivity, it helps raise your confidence, and it is a lovely moment to reflect on your day.

WIN is an acronym:

W – Win – What has been your win today? (What's gone well? What made you smile? What are you proud of?)

I – Indifferent – Is there anything that's playing on your mind, that didn't go so well today?

N – Next – What would you do differently next time?

It works like this. First of all you think back over your day from when you got up until bedtime, and you give yourself the opportunity to reflect on all that happened. I love using this strategy because half the time there has been so much going on in a day that you can easily forget all the good bits; this is the opportunity to review your day and record and respect your best bits. It's amazing how many great things happen in a day when you review it. This is you giving yourself credit for what you have done well and what you have enjoyed that day.

Now, in my experience, as soon as we give ourselves some credit or praise, a little voice comes into our head with an 'ah, but' and there is suddenly a new list of what didn't go to plan today or things we didn't get done. That's fine; we can't ignore that voice but we don't want to criticise ourselves at all – hence the next question: what hasn't gone so well? I've called this element 'indifferent' as I don't want any negative feelings attached to the things we didn't get done or that went wrong (we are human and things not going right is part of life), so we accept anything that comes up in this list.

Now onto 'next', and this is the really neat part. For anything that comes up on your indifferent list, you decide what you would or could do differently next time if it happens again, or when you will schedule what you didn't get done. What you are actually doing here is focusing on solutions and instantly you find a solution to whatever it is, and decide how you would do it differently next time, then your mind is calmed. There can be no negativity attached to a situation you have found a solution to or that you have decided to do a different way next time because you have solved it.

By completing this exercise on a daily basis you are constantly giving yourself credit and appreciating your life, while being able to let go of any negativity around events that do not go to plan because you have found a solution. This is a daily habit that should form part of your five a day for letting go of worry and fear, living in the moment and loving life.

I often find that when people introduce this strategy into their routine, initially the indifferent can outweigh the wins. But after completing it daily for a while, things soon shift and before long it's hard to come up with indifferents because the daily practice builds your confidence and self-esteem and finds solutions to problems quickly, so that within a short space of time you no longer feel any negativity around events.

I used to complete this strategy every evening on my own. Now my partner and I do it together as a natural part of our evening routine. As we climb into bed, the first question is always: what's been the best part of your day? What have been your wins?

WINning strategy

Win (what's gone well)

_____

_____

_____

Indifferent (anything that's not gone so well)

_____

_____

_____

Next (what would you do differently next time?)

_____

_____

_____

Let's talk hugs and nurture

Are you a hugger or a hand-shaker?

In the past I was definitely a hand-shaker. When I was 19, I made a really impulsive decision to go travelling for a year – first stop, Australia. Until then I hadn't really been outside my own little home town where it felt like I knew almost everyone. Travelling was incredible. I met people from all over the world with different backgrounds and experiences. One thing I noticed was how people greeted each other in such a variety of styles.

I made friends from all over Europe, different places in the UK, Canada, Thailand, New Zealand.

The new type of people for me were 'the huggers'. We didn't do much hugging in my home town. I met new friends who naturally hugged me as a greeting, and they used to tease me that hugging me was like hugging a tree. I would just stand stock still with my arms by my side and not really return the hug. However, my approach to hugs has changed massively over the years.

Studies have shown that nurturing and loving touch can reduce stress, boost heart health, help reduce fears, improve communication and reduce pain. Virginia Satir, a therapist and author known especially for her approach to family therapy, advocated hugging in her work and concluded that we need a minimum of four hugs a day for survival and eight for growth, but if you really want to grow and glow, we should aim for a dozen or more.

We have a basic need for touch and hugs help with this. If you are lucky enough to be a mum and have small children, you probably get more than your quota of hugs each day. Keep up the hugs as they grow; you're actually helping with their development and feelings of security, while boosting your own self-esteem and feeling of love.

In this chapter I am talking specifically about hugs, but many of the studies talk about other forms of physical touch, such as a comforting arm around someone's shoulders, a gentle and reassuring touch on the forearm which says, 'I'm with you,' a nurturing touch.

In 1943, psychologist Abraham Maslow created a theory of human motivation which is still referred to over 50 years later. Maslow's 'hierarchy of needs' talks of the basic human needs: 'do I have food and water?' and 'am I safe, do I have security?'. Once these more fundamental needs have been met, there are some more complex psychological needs, those that underpin our development as individuals: love, belonging, intimacy and nurture. It's these needs we meet with these strategies, to fill our love tanks, build self-esteem and love life.

Hugging outside your very close family can feel awkward though, can't it? In May 2017, just after the horrific bombing in Manchester at the Ariana Grande concert where 22 people were killed, a young Muslim man called Baktash Noori decided to stand in the centre of Manchester with a blindfold and a sign that read: 'I'm Muslim, I trust you, do you trust me enough for a hug?' He said he was so nervous at first, and then he got his first hug, then another. For a couple of days people lined up to hug Baktash; some cried. This simple act of kindness brought people together and demonstrated that people want love in this world and want to connect and care for each other. It was a brave thing to do, to stand on a street with a blindfold, and he says it is the best thing he has ever done. The hugs cost nothing, nothing at all, and yet were valuable to everyone.

We know hugs are good for us, so why don't we give more of them? Because of fear, fear of looking daft or maybe even rejection, but that of course is fear-based thinking and not coming from a place of love.

How did I embrace hugging?

I was fully introduced to the concept that hugging is good for your mind, body, soul and self-esteem when I was training in America with Jack Canfield. What I love about Jack's training is that, as well as studying the theory of his success principles, his delegates are encouraged to try the concepts out so they can feel the benefits. During this training, every day for a week all the delegates would practise hugging – we were taught how to hug! It felt pretty strange the first day, I must say, but we trusted the process, and by the end of the week these times to connect with people and give them a hug produced some incredible moments. The room always felt full of love and good vibes!

On returning to the UK, I popped into my usual sandwich shop. The team there knew I had been away training and I told them all about it. I explained I'd learnt about how important hugs were for us, and that I was now officially a hugger. I'd been working alone at home that day and hadn't had any hugs. I shared with them that we have a quota to meet, as suggested by Virginia Satir, of 12 hugs a day, and asked if anyone would like a hug. The ladies came around the counter and hugged me and then went on to tell everyone having lunch that I had free hugs to give away. It felt a little awkward but I loved the enthusiasm, and in the space of five minutes I'd reached my quota for the day. What's more, everyone who had accepted a free hug seemed to be smiling, including the window cleaner who had come into the shop to see what was going on.

I'd visit this sandwich shop twice a week, and as I approached the shop two things would happen:

1. The owner of the shop would run for the kitchen. He wasn't comfortable with hugging and, I think, would get nervous that his team might make him take part. Some people do not feel comfortable with any sort of physical touch, never mind hugging, so this must always be respected.
2. I'd enter the shop, hear the words 'it's the hugging lady' and the team behind the counter would come over for hugs, as would anyone who happened to be in the shop who wanted to join in. I would always share why we were hugging and pass on the secret to anyone joining in.

One Friday, I'd had a long day of work, it was late in the afternoon and, to be honest, I just wasn't feeling as full of the joys of spring as usual. So I chose to grab a sandwich at a different coffee shop. Sadly, I was just not in the mood for giving hugs that day. As I walked into the alternative establishment, I heard the words 'it's the hug lady' – the lady I knew from my usual place had changed jobs! She explained to all the team at the new venue that I 'did hugging' for my job (not entirely true) and she came out and gave me a huge hug. You know what? I left that place smiling and feeling so much better than when I went in. Maybe I hadn't been in the mood for giving hugs that day, but I certainly felt 100% better after having received them.

Little miracles from the universe

The last time I went to the US to work as part of Jack's assisting team, something extraordinary happened when we did the hugs section of the day, which I just want to share because if this wasn't the universe at play, I don't know what is. It is a perfect example of the little miracles that can happen when you least expect it.

It was June and Mum had passed away in January that year. The event was Jack's 'Breakthrough to Success' and the room was filled with close to five hundred people. When five hundred people in a room are silently giving each other hugs, you can imagine the beautiful energy that is produced. Anyway, I was hugging a lady I hadn't met or even seen before during the course of the week. Music was playing in the background and the song that came on was 'Fields of Gold'. This was the song we played at the service we had for Mum. I heard it and hugged and held onto the lady so tightly. She hugged me and just held me in return, and I felt a couple of tears run down my face. Because the hugs process is silent, I didn't say anything and, after a couple of minutes, I moved on to my next hug.

At lunch I saw the lady again; her name was Joanne. She approached me and said, 'I have something for you.' She gave me a pair of earrings made from feathers (not what I usually wear, to be honest) but they were white feathers and, as you know, I love a white feather – it has always meant someone who has passed away is with me. She handed me the earrings and just said: 'I don't know why. I was just having lunch and something in me told me to go and get those earrings and give them to you. I just felt you had to know that the angels are always with you.' How incredible! I am still stunned by this magical little miracle involving a lady I'd never met before but had a unique moment with. The universe at work! Little miracles happening every day.

Wishes do come true

I thought about Dad a lot when he was on his own in the house every day after Mum died. He loves a hug and I really felt for him not having hugs at hand. I could tell he was feeling down; I kept asking if he wanted a visit, but he always said he was OK. I had a full schedule and couldn't fit a long visit in for a couple of weeks.

Then one day I saw a slot in my diary and worked out that if I got up at 5.00 a.m. and drove the three hours to Dad's, I could spend half an hour with him and be back for lunchtime.

I set off and when I was about five minutes from his house, I called him and asked how he was. He said, 'Not too bad.' I said, 'I wish I could give you a hug right now,' to which he replied, 'So do I.' Then I said, 'Open the front door,' as I pulled onto the drive. We had the best hug. Hey presto! Wishes do come true.

Sometimes people won't admit it, but everyone needs more hugs – including you, the reader of this book. So I urge you to make hugging a part of your daily routine. Make it your mission to give and receive hugs every day.

For the days you are not around people to receive hugs, I have created a rather special five-minute meditation which will help you get a hug and feel the love even if you are not physically in the room with someone. We want you to have hugs, even if it's physically not possible, so this is our gift to you. Hop on over to the website www.thelipstickprinciples.co.uk and download your free hug-in-a-mug meditation today.

I can't imagine anyone getting to the end of their life and saying, 'Boy, I regret getting so many hugs.' Regret is not something we should ever have, and that's partly why I've written this book. I don't want anyone to get to the end of life, which sadly may come sooner than we can imagine, and regret not doing something or not feeling something they should have, not being confident and loving life as it is possible to.

When I adopted the core principle of living life from a place of love not fear after Mum died, I wondered if there was anything I would regret not having done if I was about to die. I thought of two things:

1. writing a book (weirdly, not this book, although in letting go of fear and writing this book I now know I can write the next, which is in fact a novel and so totally unrelated)
2. feeling completely in love, being happy inside and loving someone in a way I only dreamed was possible.

We heard earlier that Abraham Maslow stated that, to reach complete self-actualisation, we go through some basic human needs – have I got food? am I secure? – and then on to psychological needs: do I belong, have love and have intimacy? I had food, I was safe and I felt that I belonged and had love from friends and family, but intimacy wasn't there. No matter how much love you feel from friends and family, the love of a partner is something different and this part of me was hidden away, not being used. What if I got to the end of my life and never fully experienced being completely in love? I knew I had to let go of fear and open myself up to love. This is exactly what I did, I said I'm not afraid anymore, I'm ready to let love in. When I met my soul mate a few months later, the whole experience was completely different from anything that had gone before. I had no doubt, no insecurity, no fear, no worries and I let myself love and be loved in the most incredible way. This may well be how other people have always experienced relationships but it had not been that way for me. I had always worried and never loved full out, there had always been a barrier of fear of letting go completely. I will perhaps never know whether this was always going to be the one or if it was because I said no to fear and yes to love, but the fact I met him 20 years ago and ran a mile I think it's clear. Deciding to live life from a place of love not fear lets you experience life and relationships in a completely new and incredibly awesome way.

Saying 'I'm in' and living full out means embracing every part of us. Coming from a place of love not fear means we don't wrap ourselves in a blanket of protection, we're not afraid of love in case we get hurt, we're not afraid of raising our heads above the parapet in case we make a mistake, we don't just blend in to keep ourselves safe but stand up and stand out.

Are you ready to believe in the wonderful what ifs not the negative ones, to turn around negative beliefs to create positive ones, and adopt the core guiding belief of love not fear and let love in. This is what I want for you.

To fill your love tank let go of worry and fear, live in the moment and love life, start here with this LIPSTICK principle, Keep It Simple (Sweetheart) – KISS. In this chapter I have created your five a day to fill your love tank and, most importantly, love you.

Summary of the K of the LIPSTICK principles – KISS (your five a day)

1. Go on a love rampage every day with at least 19 'I love' statements, more if you want – there is no maximum. Remember we have 50,000 thoughts a day, so let's thread them with love and feed our souls. Share the love, notice people around you and what they do, and let them know why you appreciate them and what you love about what they do; make their day. Mirror mirror: connect back in and love yourself first; say 'I love you' in the mirror every evening.
2. Perform the WINning strategy every day to build your confidence. Remember and reflect on the great things, and then coach yourself on what you would do differently next time for anything that didn't go to plan.
3. Get more hugs.
4. Do a form of mindfulness or meditation every day.
5. New mantra: 'I come from a place of love not fear'.

EPILOGUE

Throughout this book you have read about lots of strategies for taking control of your life and how to let go of worry and fear, live in the moment and love life. These are the LIPSTICK principles and, just like lipstick, they need applying in order for you to feel and see the benefits. When you apply them, you will notice the change and want to do more. The more you practise and apply them, the more love you feel. The more you radiate love, the more confident you look and the more your confidence builds; as you achieve one small pot goal, you start to create bigger goals and – hey presto! – you are suddenly exactly where you once wanted to be.

By applying these principles you won't just change your world, you will change the world of the people around you. They will feel the love and want to know your secret. Share the love and the strategies with everyone. These strategies change lives. Just think how life would be if everyone was able to live with the core guiding principle of love not fear.

If you want more on the LIPSTICK principles and want to keep connected or utilise some of those fabulous meditations hop on over to the website www. thelipstickprinciples.co.uk. There is nothing I love more than hearing about what the LIPSTICK principles have done for you, so please do let me know. I can't tell you how many times in the process of writing this book I've had to reset myself from fear to love. Writing has taken me completely outside my comfort zone (much scarier than jumping out of that plane!), so if you've loved it, share the love with me. I'd love to hear from you.

And remember we have some goodies for you on the website, including meditations and the all-important hug in a mug – my way of getting a hug to you.
And finally, with love:

A Poem for the Woman That Plays the Lead Role in Her Life

When you look in the mirror, who do you see?
I wonder, do you see who I see?

I look around and see beautiful faces
Smiles that have lit up so many places
Eyes that have seen what I haven't seen
People who've been places I've never been
When you look in the mirror, who do you see?
I wonder, do you see who I see?

The leading lady, the star of your show
As you read this I want you to know
Now is the time to shine in your light
Now is the time to sparkle at night

Now is your time to know you have choices
Now is the time to hear everyone's voices
Hear all the encouragement that comes your way
All the great things people you know say
It's time to hear it and know it inside
This is your moment in which you decide
To look in the mirror and know that it's true
That reflection is perfect and it is you
The life filled with love is just a thought away
Followed by small steps and action every day
Are you ready to recognise you
And to see yourself the way others do
To step out in life and give it your all
And know there's always a net should you fall?
Remember when you jump you start flying
And we can only ever be living or dying
Now is your time, today is your day
So when you look in the mirror hear yourself say

I'm so proud of you for all you have already done
I'm so proud of you for how far you've come
I love you my friend because you are me
And at last I see what others see

When you look in the mirror, who do you see?
I hope you see the amazing lead lady
Amanda Brown

WHAT NEXT?

Book Amanda as a speaker – If you're looking for a speaker to bring the love to your next event go to: www.theleadingladiescompany.com

Say hello and follow Amanda on Instagram for more on how to apply the LIPSTICK Principles: amanda_browntllc

To join a community of women applying LIPSTICK supporting each other and loving life check out our events and programmes at: www.theleadingladiescompany.com